Princess

VICTORIA MELITA

Grand Duchess
Cyril of Russia

1876–1936

Historical biography

Frederick III: German Emperor 1888 (Alan Sutton 1981)

Queen Victoria's family: a select bibliography (Clover 1982)

Dearest Affie: Alfred, Duke of Edinburgh, Queen Victoria's second son, 1844–1900
[with Bee Jordaan] (Alan Sutton 1984)

Queen Victoria's children (Alan Sutton 1986; large print edition ISIS 1987)

Windsor and Habsburg: the British and Austrian reigning houses 1848–1922
(Alan Sutton 1987)

Edward VII's children (Alan Sutton 1989)

Music

Roxeventies: popular music in Britain 1970–79
(Kawabata 1982)

The Roy Wood story (A & F 1986)

Singles file: the story of the 45 r.p.m. record (A & F 1987)

Beyond the summertime: the Mungo Jerry story
[with Derek Wadeson] (A & F 1990)

Princess

VICTORIA
MELITA

Grand Duchess
Cyril of Russia

1876–1936

John Van der Kiste

ALAN SUTTON PUBLISHING LIMITED

First published in the United Kingdom in 1991
Alan Sutton Publishing Limited
Phoenix Mill · Far Thrupp · Stroud · Gloucestershire

First published in the United States of America in 1991
Alan Sutton Publishing Inc
83 Washington Street · Dover · NH 03820

Paperback edition first published 1994

British Library Cataloguing in Publication Data

Van der Kiste, John
Princess Victoria Melita: Grand Duchess Cyril of russia, 1876–1936
1. Russia. Royal families
I. Title
947.083092

ISBN 0–86299–815–8 (case)
ISBN 0–7509–0658–8 (paper)

Library of Congress Cataloging in Publication Data applied for

Typeset in 11/13 Baskerville.
Typesetting and origination by
Alan Sutton Publishing Limited.
Printed in Great Britain by
Hartnolls Ltd, Bodmin, Cornwall.

Contents

Illustrations

Nos. 5 and 12 appear by gracious permission of Her Majesty Queen Elizabeth II (copyright reserved). Thanks are also due to the following for kind permission to reproduce illustrations: Bayerisches Staatsarchiv, Coburg (Nos. 11, 13); Cape Archives, Cape Town (Nos. 2, 6); Det Kongelige Bibliotek, Copenhagen (Nos. 4, 7, 10, 18, 33, 34); and Mrs R. Prior, Sussex Commemorative Ware Centre, Hove, Sussex (Nos. 14, 15, 20, 21, 22, 24, 25). The remainder are from private collections.

Foreword

Of Queen Victoria's twenty-two granddaughters, none –
apart from those who were destined to become Queens or
Empresses themselves – had such a colourful life as
Princess Victoria Melita of Edinburgh, who became suc-
cessively Grand Duchess Ernest Louis of Hesse and the
Rhine, and later Grand Duchess Cyril Vladimirovich of
Russia.

Unlike so many of her contemporaries, however, her
life has never been fully documented, or given the
distinction of an individual biography. She does not
appear to have kept a journal; if so, none has survived. At
the best of times, she was an erratic letter writer, as
Queen Victoria (an indefatigable correspondent herself)
was moved to complain on more than one occasion. Even
more frustratingly, it has proved impossible to obtain
access to more than a very small amount of her surviving
correspondence.

Moreover, unlike both her husbands and her favourite
sister Marie, Queen of Roumania, she never wrote or
published any memoirs. While their reminiscences have
proved useful sources for her life, inevitably they have
tended to overshadow her life and times – a fascinating
life that began in Malta, to a childhood divided between
England, Scotland and Germany, to a married life that
took her to Germany, France and Russia, and finally a
dignified if hardly serene exile in post-war Finland,
Germany and Brittany.

After the Russian revolution in 1917 and the collapse of
imperial power, Grand Duchess Cyril seems to have been
regarded as less important. Her name features but rarely

in official records, or in *The Times*. Her activities during the last twenty years have been the subject of much speculation and gossip, often conflicting, ever since. Most people who still remember her, or who know those who can remember meeting her, are reluctant to talk about certain areas of her life, and matters such as her feelings towards the burgeoning Nazi movement are the subject of considerable disagreement.

At the risk of inconsistency, first names used throughout the text are those most commonly used in English, though they may appear in a different form when quoted in letters; for instance, Grand Duke Cyril was sometimes referred to in correspondence as Kyrill or Kirill, and where letters are used in the book the spelling remains unaltered.

I wish to acknowledge the gracious permission of Her Majesty The Queen to publish certain material of which she owns the copyright.

I am also indebted to the Hon. David Astor, by whose permission certain extracts from the correspondence of his mother, Lady Astor, to Her Majesty Queen Marie of Roumania, are published here for the first time, and to the staff, Department of Archives and Manuscripts, Reading University, for access to the material; and to Edward Voules, for permission to quote from his privately printed work *Free of all malice*.

Several people have been extremely generous with their time, their advice, and with asking other people for information. In particular, the late Mrs Bee Jordaan and John Wimbles have not only read the draft manuscript at various stages and saved me from several small factual errors, but have also been exceptionally helpful in tracking down elusive, not to say hitherto-unknown, sources of information, and with discussing various aspects of

Princess Victoria Melita's life and character. Without them, the book would have been very much harder to write; the end result is certainly very much the better for their participation.

Sadly, Bee died on 17 September 1990, shortly before this book went to press. Ever since collaborating on a biography of the Princess's father, *Dearest Affie*, published in 1984, we had considered this as a future project, and I regret that she did not live to see the final result. It is to her memory that the work is respectfully dedicated.

My thanks are also due to H.H. Prince Nicolas Romanoff; Arthur Addington; Theo Aronson; Dr Otto Hambrecht, Bayerisches Staatsarchiv, Coburg; Joyce Kilvington; Kathleen Marten, Kent State Library, Ohio, USA; Ricardo Mateos Sainz de Medrano; Aila Narva, National Archives, Helsinki, Finland; Robin Piguet; Bodil Sander, Det Kongelige Bibliotek, Copenhagen; Shirley Stapley; and, as ever, my parents, Wing Commander Guy and Nancy Van der Kiste, for their constant help, advice and encouragement during the writing of this biography.

CHAPTER 1

The Duke and Duchess of Edinburgh

A swarm of European royalty descended on St Petersburg in January 1874 for the wedding of Prince Alfred, Duke of Edinburgh, to Marie, Grand Duchess of Russia. As befitted the nuptials of a daughter of the Tsar, it was a picturesque and magnificent occasion. No less remarkable were the circumstances leading up to the marriage themselves, for in view of the fragile relations between Britain and Russia during the nineteenth century, and even more so between their reigning dynasties, it was almost unthinkable that such a match could ever come to pass.

Prince Alfred ('Affie') was born at Windsor Castle on 6 August 1844, the fourth child and second son of Queen Victoria and Prince Albert. In his formative years he compared favourably with his elder brother Prince Albert Edward ('Bertie'), Prince of Wales. While the son born to succeed his mother on the throne as King Edward VII was wilful, obstinate and given to fits of uncontrollable temper, Affie was a placid child. He was more eager to learn than his brother, and at the age of four and a half, according to his governess Lady Lyttelton, he was said to have 'very uncommon abilities; and a mind which will make the task of instructing him most smooth and delightful.'[1] His intelligence and powers of concentration were evident at an early age, as was his passion for

geography and anything to do with the Royal Navy. He
was clever with his hands, and enjoyed taking mechanical
devices to pieces and reassembling them to find out how
they worked, sometimes adding minor improvements
of his own in the process. He also made toys for the
younger children, and even a rudimentary musical
box which played *Rule Britannia,* albeit in fits and
starts.

Bertie was heir to his mother's throne; Affie was
likewise destined to succeed his Uncle Ernest as Duke of
Saxe-Coburg Gotha. Ernest had already fathered several
illegitimate children, and contracted venereal disease,
much to the disgust of his virtuous brother Albert. It
seemed unlikely that he and his wife Alexandrine would
produce an heir to the duchy. The succession would
therefore fall to Affie. Yet he could not be educated
entirely abroad; should anything happen to Bertie, he
would be King, and as Prince Albert pointed out to his
brother, 'if we make a German of him, it might be very
difficult for him and for our country.'[2]

At the age of eleven, Affie began training for the Royal
Navy under the supervision of a tutor, Lieutenant John
Cowell. Three years later, he passed his entrance examin-
ation with excellent marks, and spent much of the next
three years away from home, apart from occasional
periods of leave with the family at Windsor, Osborne and
Balmoral.

During his formative years, Affie showed signs of
growing up to be very like his father. He was never bored;
his perpetually-inquiring mind and busy hands meant
that he could always find himself something to do, and he
was happy to be left on his own. Inevitably this went with
a tendency to be quiet and rather shy, a trait sometimes
mistaken for rudeness in later life by those who did not
know him better. In character he was remarkably unlike
Bertie, an extrovert who relished the company of others,

and never liked being left to his own devices, and hated books or anything remotely connected with the school-room. The brothers were devoted to each other, and this fraternal bond would last throughout their lives, but people outside the family readily observed how different they were. Charles Wynne-Carrington, chosen to come and play as a boy at Eton with them while the family was in residence at Windsor, remarked that he liked the Prince of Wales much better, even though Prince Alfred 'was the favourite'.

Father and second son also shared a common bond in their love for Coburg. On his visits to Uncle Ernest and Aunt Alexandrine, Affie realized that he found the same feelings of contentment and tranquillity at Rosenau, the birthplace of Prince Albert who always retained a great affection for the castle.

However, Affie was to be deprived of his father's guidance at an early age. A few weeks after his seven-teenth birthday and one glorious family holiday in the Scottish Highlands, Affie sailed from Liverpool to join the North American and West Indies station. Several thousand miles away that winter, his grieving relations at Windsor gathered round the bed of the Prince Consort. Prince Albert, gravely weakened by overwork and anxiety, had aged far beyond his forty-two years, and on 14 December 1861 he succumbed to an attack of typhoid. Apart from his eldest sister Vicky, Crown Princess of Prussia, recovering from pneumonia at Berlin, Affie was the only one of the children not at Windsor. Not until February 1862 did he arrive home on an extended period of compassionate leave. Ironically his efforts to be cheer-ful, and his reluctance to observe every little detail of mourning at home, began to drive mother and son apart. Much as he missed his father, and was saddened at being denied the solace of relations at the time, he argued that he was trying not to be heartless. With the resilience of youth, he knew that life had to go on; but the brave face he showed to the family was not appreciated in what had become a house of deepest mourning.

Worse was to come. That summer Affie rejoined his ship and sailed for Malta. Queen Victoria had asserted, somewhat hysterically, that an affair between the Prince of Wales and an actress in Ireland the previous year had 'broken her Angel's beloved heart'. Now, when their second son likewise yielded to the temptations of the opposite sex, and rumours of an affair he had had on Malta reached her, she was shocked by his 'heartless and dishonourable behaviour'.

This had happened at a rather inopportune moment. The Greeks had just rebelled against their unpopular and childless King Otto, and the provisional government was asking the protecting powers of Britain, France and Russia to nominate a candidate for the vacant throne. Although members of these three countries' ruling families were ineligible under the terms of a London protocol signed in 1830, the Greeks showed great enthusiasm for 'a son of Queen Victoria', it was reported cryptically in the press. By mid-November it was apparent that Prince Alfred's election as King of the Hellenes was almost a foregone conclusion. In a plebiscite held at the end of the year, he received over 95 per cent of the votes cast. Yet much to his relief, the British government made it clear that he was not permitted to accept the throne, and at length a prince of the Danish house of Glucksburg was chosen instead.

In 1866 Affie was promoted to the rank of Captain, and three months later Queen Victoria created him Duke of Edinburgh, and Earl of Ulster and Kent. By the end of the year, plans were well under way for him to take his ship HMS *Galatea* on a world cruise. It was a responsibility which, the Queen remarked coldly, he seemed to view 'with such reluctance and suspicion'. He was unhappy at the idea of being separated from family and friends for so long, but this was just what she wanted, hoping that 'the responsibility and the separation from his London flatterers will do him good.'³ He had shown a marked predilection for society life, and the Queen feared that he was too infatuated with his charming sister-in-law, Princess Alexandra.

All the same, he discharged his duties on the world cruise with distinction, though a lengthy sojourn in Australia soon palled for him. It was, however, cut short when an attempt on his life was made near Sydney in March 1868. A Fenian sympathizer, seeking revenge for the execution of three members of the Fenian Brotherhood for shooting a policeman in Manchester, found the nearby presence of Queen Victoria's second son a providential target for revenge. Affie was shot and wounded in the back, but fortunately the bullet was deflected from his spine by a pair of heavy braces, and removed after a short operation. He returned home, where he quickly exhausted his mother's patience by receiving 'ovations as if he had done something – instead of God's mercy having spared his life.'⁴ A second cruise on *Galatea* took him to India, Asia and the South American continent, and he returned in May 1871.

Shortly before setting sail again at the end of 1868, he had stayed at Jugenheim with his sister Alice and her husband Prince Louis of Hesse and the Rhine. Several other members of the Russian and Hessian families were present, among them Grand Duchess Marie, fourteen-year-old daughter of Alexander II, Tsar of Russia. It was this same Marie, the Duke told his mother shortly after completing his travels in 1871, that he wished to marry.

Her Imperial Highness the Grand Duchess Marie Alexandrovna was born on 17 October 1853, sixth child

of Tsarevich Alexander and the former Princess Marie of
Hesse and the Rhine. There were six sons of the marriage, all of whom lived to maturity, and two daughters.
The elder, Alexandra, had died in infancy, and as the
only surviving girl, Marie was inevitably the apple of her
father's eye. She grew up to be rather spoilt, used to
having her own way, and as a result of being surrounded
by brothers, somewhat brusque and masculine in her
demeanour. Certainly she inherited nothing of her
mother's fragile beauty.

Marie's eldest brother, Tsarevich Nicholas, died
shortly after being betrothed to Princess Dagmar of
Denmark, sister of the Princess of Wales. It was
Nicholas's dying wish that Dagmar should marry his
brother Alexander, and the match was a very happy one.
Both Danish-born sisters and Princess Louis of Hesse,
Queen Victoria's second daughter, were anxious to ease
tension and suspicion between their adopted countries,
and to this end they arranged regular meetings of British,
German and Russian royalty with the annual Danish
family reunions. King Christian IX and Queen Louise
were supremely fortunate in having such a united family.
Queen Victoria, used to pacifying warring elements
between her sons and daughters when continental marriages, divided loyalties, and Bismarck's policy of blood
and iron exacted their toll on fraternal harmony,
remarked with envy on how King Christian's brood 'never
breathe one word against each other, and the daughters
remain as unspoilt and as completely Children of the
Home as when they were unmarried'.[5]

It was at one such meeting that Affie and Marie came
face to face for the first time. Marie was not yet fifteen, so
it was hardly a case of love at first sight. Nonetheless Affie
liked her company and thought she had plenty of character. No less importantly, he realized that once he
returned from the second part of his cruise on *Galatea*

(which he was scheduled to join again a few weeks hence), Queen Victoria would increase pressure on him to consider a suitable marriage. He had already been more than mildly infatuated with his sister-in-law, and after that with Lady Constance Grosvenor, Duchess of Westminster. The Queen knew that the sooner a wife was found for him the better, and preferably a German one.

Having allowed her eldest son to marry a Danish princess had, in her eyes, proved a grave miscalculation for political reasons. Within less than a year of the marriage, Germany and Denmark had gone to war over the future of the Schleswig-Holstein duchies. Despite the Queen's steadfast German sympathies, the Prince and Princess of Wales had – without actively trying – helped to swing public opinion at large firmly on the side of beleaguered Denmark.

Several German princesses had been considered for Affie, but ruled out for various reasons, mainly on grounds of health or total lack of mutual attraction. Princess Elizabeth of Wied came the closest to becoming Duchess of Edinburgh, but her eccentricities were revealed when she discovered that her suitor played the violin. When he was invited to stay with the family, she and her mother organized an expedition into their favourite beech woods, so that he could serenade them under the trees. Gallantly he complied with this strange command – he could hardly say no – but he vowed silently between clenched teeth that he would never marry anyone with such peculiar notions.

If there were no eligible German princesses for Affie, why not a Romanov Grand Duchess? The Princess of Wales, her sister, and his sister Alice all thought that such a dynastic union would help to further the cause of European harmony, and ease relations between England and Russia. As the Tsar's only daughter, Marie would doubtless come into a considerable fortune on her marriage, and Affie had

inherited something of the Coburg parsimony. Sir John
Cowell, now his secretary, maintained that his concern with
money 'amounted to a disease'. On her side, Marie was
fascinated by this deeply-tanned sailor prince and Duke
with a wealth of stories about his recent world travels,
comprising what was probably the most extensive journey
yet undertaken by a European prince – and with a wound in
his back, to bear witness to the most hair-raising episode of
them all.

Affie's meeting with Tsar Alexander II in July 1871
proved to be a prelude to two years' difficult courtship.
The Tsar and Tsarina dreaded the idea of losing their
beloved daughter to a foreign court, and hoped fervently
that a prince who would stay in Russia might be found for
her. As for Queen Victoria, she had no love for the
Romanovs, whom she regarded as 'false and arrogant'.
According to her great-grandson, Earl Mountbatten of
Burma, speaking a century later, 'she feared Russia, with
very good reason. She had the view . . . that absolute
autocracy was wrong and was bound to end in tears,
which it did.'[6]

A contemporary of Mountbatten, Tsar Alexander's
granddaughter Grand Duchess Olga, had no doubt of
Queen Victoria's feelings for the family: 'Victoria was
always contemptuous of us. She said that we possessed a
"bourgeoisie", as she called it, which she disliked
intensely. . . . My father (Tsar Alexander III) could not
stand her. He said that she was a pampered, sentimental,
selfish old woman.'[7]

Less than twenty years had elapsed since the English
and French armies had gone to war with Russia in the
Crimea, and mutual emnity was still just below the
surface. Religious differences posed another obstacle,
until the Queen was assured that members of the Greek
Orthodox church (to which the Romanovs belonged) did
not refuse to acknowledge any creed other than their own,

unlike Roman Catholics. She accepted that the choice of wives for her second son was becoming so narrow that they 'must get over the difficulties concerning religion'.

More than once, Queen Victoria believed that what she called 'the Russian project' was over. She heard from various sources that the Grand Duchess was too deeply attached to her home; the Tsar and Tsarina would not let her marry, except to a Russian; and later that she was in disgrace for having had an affair with one Russian officer and regular correspondence with another. At one stage, she insisted that there must be 'mutual attachment' between the Duke of Edinburgh and the Grand Duchess, and that they must marry within the year, 'or else it must finally be put an end to'.

At length patience brought its own reward. On 11 July 1873 at Jugenheim, Affie asked for Marie's hand, and she accepted him. When she received his telegram in which he told her how happy they were, and 'hoping that your blessings rest on us', the Queen at Osborne professed astonishment 'at the great rapidity with which the matter has been settled and announced'. To Vicky, she wrote bluntly, 'The murder is out!'

The Duke of Edinburgh and Grand Duchess Marie were married at St Petersburg on 23 January 1874, at a double ceremony. The first was performed according to the Greek Orthodox Church, the second according to the rites of the Church of England. It was the only marriage among Queen Victoria's children which she did not attend in person, but she sent Arthur Stanley, Dean of Westminster, to perform the English service. Lady Stanley was commanded to report back to her sovereign in full detail.

Bride and groom arrived at Windsor on a sunny day in March. At last the Queen had repented of her persistently churlish attitude, and relished this first chance to meet her son's bride. Though she had to admit that the Duchess of Edinburgh was not pretty or graceful, and held herself rather badly, she was 'most pleasingly natural, unaffected and civil; very sensible and frank'. Best of all, she was 'not a bit afraid of Affie and I hope will have the very best influence upon him'.[8]

Yet Queen Victoria's apprehensions about having a Romanov daughter-in-law were soon justified. Marie and the Tsar informed the Queen that she was to be known as Her Imperial Highness, 'as in all civilised countries'. This rankled with the not yet imperial Queen* who retorted that she did not mind whether her daughter-in-law was called Imperial or not, as long as the style Royal came first. Then there were arguments as to which title should come first, when referring to Marie – Grand Duchess of Russia, or Duchess of Edinburgh? Feeling out of her depth on the matter, the Queen referred it to her private secretary Sir Henry Ponsonby, who was amused at so much fuss about such trivialities, and quoted Dr Johnson to his wife: 'Who comes first, a louse or a flea?'.

In May 1874 Tsar Alexander paid a state visit to England. This coincided with another argument about Marie's position at court. It rankled with her that as an emperor's daughter she was not granted right of precedence over the Princess of Wales, by birth the mere daughter of a King of Denmark. The Tsar had to concede to Queen Victoria that Princess Alexandra should indeed precede Marie, as wife of the heir to the throne, but he asked for his daughter to take precedence over her other sisters-in-law. This the Queen would not countenance, but Marie exacted her own subtle revenge. At her first

*Not until her proclamation as Empress of India in 1877 could she be considered 'truly imperial'.

drawing-room she took malicious pleasure in showing off her splendid jewellery. The English princesses could not hide their jealousy, while the Queen looked at the pearls and diamonds disdainfully 'shrugging her shoulders like a bird whose plumage has been ruffled, her mouth drawn down at the corners in an expression which those who knew her had learned to dread'.[9]

Despite her readiness to criticize, Queen Victoria was never slow to give praise where it was due. She realized that nothing could be done about the Duchess of Edinburgh's shortcomings. Like those of her son, they had to be accepted, and the best made of all positive qualities. Marie, she acknowledged, had 'a kind and indulgent disposition, free from bigotry and intolerance, and her serious, intelligent mind – so entirely free from everything fast – and so full of occupation and interest in everything makes her a most agreeable companion. Everyone must like her.'[10]

Hardly anybody did. Marie found England a bitter disappointment. She thought London 'an impossible place, people are mad of pleasure', English food abominable, late hours very tiring, and visits to Windsor and Osborne boring beyond belief. Compared to the finery of St Petersburg, Buckingham Palace and Windsor Castle were drab and unappealing. She made no effort to like or see anything good in her new surroundings, or to endear herself to family and servants.

The contrast with her sister-in-law was acute. Although prematurely deaf, invariably unpunctual, and where her children were concerned very possessive, the Princess of Wales was attractive, graceful, charming, and popular with the family. The most that could be said against her was that she was not an intellectual, and certainly not clever; and to the English who had deprecated the late Prince Consort's zest for knowledge and earnestness of purpose, such shortcomings were a positive virtue. The

Duchess of Edinburgh was intelligent, extremely well-educated, and spoke several languages fluently. At the same time she was dowdy, brusque, plain, and arrogant. She rightly gave the impression that she cared nothing for what people thought of her. It was just as well, for the time would come when she was known behind her back as the most unpopular member of royalty in England. Her imperious treatment of servants, and her defiance of convention by smoking cigarettes in public, only enhanced her bad reputation.

Unfortunately Affie was no help. Unlike the outgoing Prince of Wales, he found it difficult to make friends, and his personality did not inspire confidence in others. He was an active patron of music, and among his friends and admirers was Sir Arthur Sullivan, under whose influence the Duke lent his active support for the foundation of the Royal College of Music at South Kensington. Since boyhood he had played the violin, though it was said that his prowess was overrated, and grew ever more uncertain with age. Moreover he was inclined to be taciturn when sober, and a loquacious bore after a few drinks. To the Duchess, his faults could be blamed on his 'thoroughly English education'.

Shortly after the wedding, Marie was asked rather bluntly when the first baby would appear. With uncharacteristic good humour, she replied that she was in no hurry, but Alfred was very impatient. Barely nine months after the marriage ceremonies she gave birth to a son, also named Alfred, on 15 October 1874, at Buckingham Palace. One year later, at their country home, Eastwell Park, near Ashford, Kent, she presented him with a daughter, Marie.

Clarence House, London, was the official residence of the Edinburghs, but it was too formal and lacked privacy. In any case, Marie hated London, and Affie was no less keen to have a home where they were less exposed to the public gaze – and further away from the eagle eye of Queen Victoria, even though she too spent as little time in her capital as possible.

Eastwell Park was rented from the Earl of Winchelsea. It was a massive pretentious grey bulk of mock-Tudor, with grounds of 2,500 acres overlooking Romney Marsh. The estates included rich woodland and rolling parks, with Highland cattle and deer. Every autumn Affie invited large shooting parties to make full use of the facilities. With her love of cultured and intellectual company, Marie disliked these sporting seasons intensely. She complained that after a day out with their guns, the men returned sleepy and in no mood for interesting conversation.

In February 1876 the Duke of Edinburgh was appointed to the command of HMS *Sultan*. After spending several months in her in home waters as a unit of the Channel Fleet, he transferred to the Mediterranean fleet, based on Malta. The ducal couple made San Antonio Palace on Malta their official winter residence.

Here, on 25 November 1876, Marie gave birth to a second daughter. She was named firstly after her maternal grandmother, and secondly after her birthplace. Princess Victoria Melita, to be known *en famille* throughout her life as 'Ducky', had thus bestowed a singular honour on the Mediterranean island. The local press observed proudly that 'Malta now claims the honour of being the birth-place of a Royal child. No other colony in Her Majesty's broad possessions can claim the same.'[11]

CHAPTER 2

'This passionate, often misunderstood child'

*T*hroughout childhood, Ducky's closest companion was her elder sister Marie, 'Missy'. As the latter related in her memoirs, they were inseparable, though very different both in looks and character. Ducky was darker, taller, and therefore always assumed by others to be the elder, a misapprehension which annoyed them both. She was more serious, and inclined to be resentful when reproved; 'she also loved jealously and was what our elders called a "difficult child".'[1] Missy was more easy-going, extroverted, and made friends easily. Shy and sensitive, Ducky took after her father in character. She was the favourite of their Scottish nurse, who had great sympathy for 'this passionate, often misunderstood child'. But there was no jealousy between the sisters; 'we always played the game and never wanted to have separate successes; we could not conceive of a life where we should not be side by side.'[2]

In due course, there would be four sisters in the nursery. Alexandra Victoria ('Sandra') was born on 1 September 1878, and Beatrice ('Baby Bee') on 20 April 1884. Their formative years were happy and carefree, 'the childhood of rich, healthy children protected from the buffets and hard realities of life'.

'Three of us sisters were born leaders, but each in quite a different way,' Missy wrote in later life. 'I used gentleness and a deep understanding of the other man's side of the case. Ducky used strength and withering contempt when disappointed ... We were a strong race; the mixture of Russian and English was a strange blend, setting us somewhat apart from the others, as, having strong and dominating characters, we could not follow, only lead.'[3]

The Duke of Edinburgh was not often at home, for naval duties occupied much of his time. To the children, 'he was even a little bit of a stranger', although a good-looking stranger at that, with his tanned skin and deep blue eyes. They were a little in awe of him, but 'the days when he paid attention to us were red-letter days.'

Their mother had by far the greater influence on their lives. They always turned to Mama for help, she took them out for walks and drives, told them what they were allowed or forbidden to do, and came to kiss them goodnight. Her children were 'the supreme and central interest of her existence', but she was a stern, Spartan parent. A born conversationalist, she declared that nothing was more hopeless than a princess who never opened her mouth. When her children were invited out for a meal, they must never refuse what was set before them, as to do so would be an insult to their hostess. If the food made them feel sick, they could be sick – as long as they waited until they got home. They must never complain of ill-health; neither colds, headaches, nor fevers should prevent them from carrying on as normal.

Inevitably, she compared her Russian upbringing favourably with prevailing English fashions. English doses for the merest indisposition were much stronger than a continental dose; they were 'des remedes de cheval'. As for food, the English spoilt their digestion from earliest childhood by imagining that they could not eat this or that, whereas in Russia, nobody ever spoke about digestion, 'a most unpleasant subject and not drawing-room conversation'.

The Duchess's main help at home was her old maid

Fanny Renwick, a dark woman with a moustache (according to Missy) who claimed that Spanish blood flowed in her veins. A mercurial woman whose mood would change without warning, she was alternately loved and hated by the youngsters. She looked after the Duchess's wardrobe and stocks of all that her mistress's eccentricities would ever need in the way of provisions. Chief among these were vast quantities of castor-oil pills, 'that looked like transparent white grapes with the oil moving about inside', ordered, naturally, from St Petersburg. So many arrived at a time that most of them dried up in their boxes before they could be used.

Eastwell, where the children spent the winter months, was their favourite home. To them the house seemed huge, so vast that they never succeeded in exploring all the rooms. The gardens and park also provided endless places to play, and when they discovered a hollow tree with a large hole in it – so large that all three elder sisters and their brother could sit inside at once – their delight knew no bounds.

The Duke of Edinburgh was more at ease with his contemporaries, and the role of playful father did not come naturally to him. However, he particularly enjoyed playing one special game with his children on winter evenings at Eastwell. The lamps were extinguished, and he would hide in a dark corner, pretending to be an ogre. The youngsters, never knowing which room he was in, would crawl through the rooms in pitch darkness, and just when they thought all 'danger' was over, he would catch them off their guard and suddenly spring out, his growls and their hysterical shrieks of laughter ringing through the passages.

Christmas was always spent at Eastwell, and like his father before him, the Duke keenly anticipated the hours of preparation that went into the festivities. With the zest of a boy himself, he supervised every little detail – putting up a tree in the library, laying out presents on white-covered tables placed against the walls, and getting everyone to take turns in stirring the servants' plum pudding. The climax came on Christmas Eve, when family and servants were called to watch the library doors thrown open to reveal the tree in a blaze of candlelight and fragrance of singed fir branches, everyone gasping with wonder as gifts were distributed.

The children thoroughly disliked London, and it was always a wrench to leave the joys of the Kent countryside for the grimy city atmosphere at Clarence House. Admittedly there were compensations, like being allowed to play in the gardens at Buckingham Palace, with their 'delightful mysterious corners' and the lake. What they really dreaded were gloomy walks in Green Park, where there was no privacy, no sense of mystery, to compensate for the London 'smuts'. Any fall on London soil 'meant black stains on clothes, knees or stockings', and had 'a special greasiness'.

Each summer, the young Edinburghs stayed at Osborne Cottage on the Isle of Wight. Ducky and her sisters would always cherish their memories of Osborne as synonymous with summer holidays, the delights of sea and seashore, fascinating shells to be found and collected at low tide, bathing, and drives through sweet-smelling hedges full of honeysuckle. Even the Duchess of Edinburgh was content on the island; it was perhaps the only part of Britain which escaped her censure.

Another great attraction of Osborne was that the girls could run wild around the gardens, without their governess to keep them in order. The Duchess engaged a French tutor, primarily to coach young Alfred, but also to help her daughters to polish up their command of the tongue. He would have been better suited to his post if he could have climbed trees as well, for they were forever climbing up trees to escape from him and his dreaded *dictées*.

One summer they went to Balmoral instead, staying initially at Abergeldie Maines with their governess. That autumn, the Duchess joined them and they went to Birkhall, 'a rather bigger house or cottage' on the Balmoral estate, lent them by the Queen. Although their memories of the place always remained hazy, Missy could just recall that the rooms were so small that the three elder girls had to sleep together in one bed, two with their heads towards the top, the other with her head against the foot to separate them. Most of Queen Victoria's family disliked or were soon bored by the Scottish countryside, but the young Edinburgh princesses adored the mysterious terrain with its moors and burns, its mists and lochs, and above all the heather, 'that wonderful rolling carpet of purple, with an undergrowth of rust, which added that warmth of colour which so completely satisfied the beauty-loving eye'.[4]

When they were children, meeting Queen Victoria herself was always a special occasion. She followed their development with grandmotherly affection, but also 'with the anxious severity of one who wished that those of her House should do it every honour, no matter where they were placed'. The nurses would take the girls to see the awe-inspiring little lady in her crinoline-like black silk dresses and white widow's cap, walking silently through soft-carpeted corridors, 'like a troop of well-behaved little geese'. Grandmama and children were always tongue-tied on these occasions, and of conversation between them there was little; but 'inquiry as to our morals and general behaviour made up a great part of it,' Missy recalled, 'and I well remember Grandmama's shocked and yet amused little exclamations of horror when it was reported that one or the other of us had not been good.' There was unspoken relief on all sides when these audiences were over.

The contrast between life in Britain and Russia was

acute. All the Edinburgh children were quick to notice how much more at home their mother seemed in the land of her birth than in that of their father, and it was Ducky who took after her mother in developing a decided preference for the world of her Romanov ancestors. Russia meant colossal palaces, wonderful parks, fountains and gardens, vast family gatherings, military displays, and religious ceremonies in churches that glittered with gold. Everywhere in the imperial palaces there was a special odour, synonymous with Russia; a mixture of turpentine, Russian leather, cigarette smoke and scent, uniquely characteristic. It was a fairy-like, legendary atmosphere, an irresistible yet fragile glamour, soon to be swept away by the events of the early twentieth century.

When Ducky paid her first visit as a small girl to St Petersburg, the court was presided over by her grandfather Tsar Alexander II, a giant of a man with grey hair and closely-cut whiskers, a rather forbidding face but kindly eyes and mouth, which could not however conceal a perpetual expression of worry. The Tsarina they saw very rarely. Already an invalid, with only a few years to live, she was bedridden, and her place in her husband's affections had been taken by his mistress, Katherine Dolgorouky. The Romanov Grand Dukes looked equally forbidding, tall, bewhiskered and uniformed, but they spoilt their young half-English nieces unashamedly, showering them with endless gifts of sweets and jewellery.

Ducky, Missy and their sisters came in for much gentle teasing from their uncles and aunts in Britain and Russia. As adults, Queen Victoria's children had a strange habit of starting conversations with their nieces and nephews and then wandering off absent-mindedly, or looking through them as if they were simply not there. But the Grand Dukes and Duchesses at Moscow and St Petersburg always gave the impression of being more attentive and responsive to their young visitors' interests and needs.

For the first few years, the Edinburgh children were kept carefully shielded from the stark realities of the revolutionary undercurrents that undermined their Mama's family. But one morning in March 1881 they were horrified to find the Duchess kneeling in her room at Clarence House, in floods of tears. While returning from a military review in St Petersburg, the Tsar had been assassinated by a nihilist's bomb. Several times during the preceding years he had been hounded and chased by the revolutionaries, with soldiers and servants having met their end with bombs intended for their sovereign. At length, they had succeeded.

Although they found it hard to grieve for a grandfather whom they had barely known, the intensity of their mother's grief – Mama, who had always seemed so strong and invincible – presented them with a salutary first lesson in human vulnerability.

Queen Victoria fondly preserved the correspondence from her many grandchildren, and the earliest surviving letter to her from Ducky is a note wishing her a happy birthday in May 1882. Various thank-you letters for birthday and Christmas presents, and one acknowledging the gift of £2 for teeth, emanated from Clarence House and Eastwell Park. Significantly the first ones are in French. The Duchess of Edinburgh, who despised the English language as being as ugly as the country, much preferred the French tongue, and evidently her children were brought up to express themselves thus. Not until she was eight years of age did Ducky apparently start writing to Grandmama in English.

A note from Balmoral (26 November 1885) records the presents she received for her ninth birthday:

I write to thank you very much for your pretty
present, and for your nice letter. I got lots of
presents as well as a beautiful doll's house. It was
raining very much in the morning and so we had
great fun indors [sic], it is almost as nasty today. I
think you would like to know all I got for my
birthday. From Mama and Papa I got the doll's
house, and a little china picture, and a brooch.
From sister I got a paint box and a little scent
bottle and from Alfred a bracket with a deers head,
and some other things . . . [5]

In January 1886 the Duke of Edinburgh was appointed
Commander-in-Chief of the Mediterranean squadron,
based on Malta. The island, which had been their official
winter residence for one brief season – when Ducky was
born – was to be their home again during the winter
months for three years, and in October the royal yacht
Osborne steamed into the harbour at Valletta with the
Duchess and her daughters on board.

San Antonio was the governor's summer palace. On
installing themselves there that autumn, the youngsters
found something to delight them in every corner – the
house with its huge stone-paved rooms and rocky garden
containing a walled-in oasis, secret and eastern-looking,
with a maze of trees; jasmine, knee-high geraniums,
verbena, masses of roses, large clumps of feathery white
chrysanthemums tumbling in snowy cascades; violets,
narcissi and anemones in great quantity. Whenever the
fleet was in Malta the Duke lived ashore with them,
travelling between ship and shore in a ten-oared galley he
had had specially built.

The Duchess was glad to leave Eastwell Park for the
last time, for at San Antonio she could be mistress of all
she surveyed for a while, far from the all-pervading
presence of her mother-in-law. The princesses would tear

around the island on small Barbary Arab ponies. It was difficult to keep them out of the stables, where they would often be found elbow-deep in bran mash, helping the stable hands. 'Our ideas about riding were anything but civilized,' Missy recalled. 'We were entirely fearless and our chief pace was full gallop, quite regardless of the ground.'[6] Many a poor governess was led a fine dance keeping up with them.

Ducky described her tenth birthday celebrations in a letter to Queen Victoria (27 November 1886), thanking her for the gift of a watch:

> I got all my presents before breakfast. After, we
> went to spend the day at St Paul's Bay, it was a
> very fine day so that Missy and I rode, it took us
> nearly two hours to get there and we enjoyed
> ourselves very much, Mama invited two officers
> from Papa's ship to ride with us, Mademoiselle
> rode too. We had luncheon in a house near there,
> and then we went in a little boat to the little island
> where St Paul's ship was wrecked. We got out of
> the boats and walked over the island, but there
> was nothing to see in it, it was a bare rock with
> only the statue of St Paul. We came back from the
> island and then we started home, we had hardly
> started when it began to rain very hard and before
> we got home we were all wet through. The weather
> is very cool but fine.[7]

One month later, Ducky wrote (28 December 1886) to describe the seasonal festivities on Malta:

> I thank you so much for the very pretty cross you
> sent me, please thank aunt Beatrice for her nice
> card. I hope very much you will like the little
> table-cloth we worked for you. We had a very

happy Christmas and we are going to have
holidays till the 3rd of January. This evening there
will be a lottery for the servants and we are also
going to cut the Xmas tree. There have been a
great many races here and we have been to see
them all. On the 1st of January we are going to a
party on board the Alexandra, there will be
dancing, a pantomime and a wild beast show of
people dressed up.[8]

From time to time there were visits to the ancestral
home at Coburg. A letter from Ducky (22 May 1887)
which accompanied the sisters' birthday present to
Queen Victoria recorded that:

We had a very nice journey from Malta here, we
stopped on the way at Naples where we saw a
great many things, at Florence and Munich. Alfred
was very pleased to see us again, and we were very
pleased to see him. We went to the market
yesterday with big baskets and bought a lot of
plants for our little gardens. Uncle of Coburg is
here now. We go sometimes to the theatre here,
because it begins and finishes very early.[9]

There was another reason why Ducky and Missy would
long remember those three years on Malta. Their cousin
Prince George of Wales was serving as fifth Lieutenant in
the Mediterranean fleet. Very homesick and missing
dreadfully the company of his parents and sisters at
Sandringham, he was soon put at ease by the solicitude of
his uncle's family. The Duke of Edinburgh had great
affection for his nephew with whom he had much in
common. They shared a love of philately, shooting, and of
course the Royal Navy. Ironically the Duke seemed more
fond of him than of his own son, who had been handed

over at the age of nine to a bullying German tutor, to be brought up in Coburg as her eventual Duke. The Duchess also liked George, and while he was in Malta, he found that she was almost 'like a second mother' to him. Although ten years older than Missy, his sheltered life had kept him a very young twenty-one, and he was 'not a bit too grand and grown up' to be the best of friends with her and her sisters. While she might regard him as a 'beloved chum', he was not alone in thinking that their relationship might go further than that.

To Prince George, his Edinburgh cousins were 'the dear three'; and they would ride together on their ponies, or in a high two-wheeled dog cart drawn by Cocky, a brown cob. On occasions the whole family would attend the carnival parades in Valletta, but it was not an agreeable experience, as the people pelted them with sugar plums. All of them were hit in the face and on the head, and Prince Alfred, home on one of his rare vacations from Coburg, got one in his eye. 'I have seen enough of that rot to last me a life time',[10] Prince George remarked succinctly.

If Missy was generally the first of the girls to make an impression on other members of the family, because of her long fair hair and outgoing demeanour, Ducky too attracted attention as she was so much her opposite. After Queen Victoria came to visit the Duke (who had returned to England, suffering from 'Maltese remittent fever') and his family at Clarence House in May 1889, she recorded in her journal that Ducky was 'nearly as tall as her mother, and such a handsome girl'.[11]

Princess Louis of Battenberg, a cousin whose husband also served in the Mediterranean fleet, had ample opportunity to observe the girls. She often took the three elder ones for a gallop on their ponies around the island. Missy, she remarked, was 'a remarkably pretty girl'; Sandra 'a chubby little thing'; and Ducky 'somewhat farouche, as she was shy'.[12]

When Ducky was twelve, her father's command at Malta came to an end and the family moved to Coburg. Now they could be closer to 'young Alfred', as they installed themselves at the Palais Edinburg. 'Uncle Coburg', the dissolute and ageing brother of the Prince Consort, was in his early seventies, and could not be expected to live for much longer.

At last, the Duchess of Edinburgh could see to it that her daughters as well as her son were brought up as 'good Germans'. For the imperial Germany of 1889 was no longer as close to the heart of Queen Victoria and her family as the German confederation of the 1840s and 1850s that Prince Albert had once hoped would be united under a more peaceful and liberal Prussia. Inclined towards Germany from an early age, largely through her mother, the Duchess naturally espoused the German cause. Even so, she and her husband kept their distance from the unspeakable Duke Ernest.

The Duke of Edinburgh cared little for the dull, boring day-to-day existence at Coburg, its sporting facilities apart, and he was grateful that naval and representative duties allowed him to spend no more than a few weeks there at a time. It did not escape general notice that the Duke and Duchess appeared to be spending less and less time together.

The Duchess held court at the Palais Edinburg. The autocratic Romanov in her preferred the freedom of a German state to a country house in England where Queen Victoria was never far away. 'She was her own mistress; it was a small kingdom perhaps, but her will was undiscussed, she took her orders from no one, and could live as she wished.'[13] The years in which she had

been based at Malta, travelling to every corner of Europe
and Russia as she pleased, had given her a taste of
independence which she did not intend to relinquish by
returning to England.

Ducky was developing into a thoughtful, serious
personality. Missy recalled how the roles she chose in
their games and improvised *tableaux* together revealed
this sister's character:

> Ducky usually played the part of my husband, my
> son or my horse, or all three in turn, according to
> the necessities of the game.
>
> Ducky always played the heroic, brave, self-
> sacrificing parts, and was almost always a male.
> There was something heroic about Ducky, even at
> that early age; something a little sombre. She was
> the one who espoused causes, she was the 'fore-
> fighter', the one who discussed and resented, who
> allowed no nonsense, and had no patience with
> frauds. She immediately spotted any insincerity
> and let nothing pass. Tall for her age, she was
> strong and rebellious, but like the strong she was
> also a defender of the weak and oppressed, and
> sometimes she even espoused lost causes with a
> bravery that we less heroic ones admired without
> imitating.
>
> I on the contrary was always inclined to let well
> alone.[14]

As for Sandra, she was 'a fat, harmless child, sweet-
tempered and fair-haired', who – luckily for the cause of
peace in the nursery – followed her elder sisters' foot-
steps, 'eager but humble before reproof'. They treated
her, by their own admission, 'with a certain imperious
offhandedness which had no unkindness in it, but which
overruled her timid desires, offering her the parts she was

to play in such wise that she could not but accept them.'

Missy and Ducky took their lessons together. The subjects included geography, history, arithmetic, botany, literature, religion, natural history, painting, French, music and gymnastics. Their educational regime does not seem to have been a severe one, despite the number of subjects, and only years later did it dawn on them that their schooling had been very sketchy. Ducky made the better pupil of the two; she was more quick-witted, eager to learn, had a more retentive memory, and was better at spelling. She was also less ready to accept facts at face value, and with her keen and enquiring mind she relished arguing, not for its own sake so much as out of a desire to question things.

For the princesses, life at Coburg 'had its own special charm; it was simple and easy.' Ducky's birthday letter to Queen Victoria (20 May 1889) describes a visit to nearby Sonneberg to buy her some toys to give their young cousins, Princess Beatrice's children, and other summer activities:

> The theatre has come back now and we are very
> pleased because it is a great pleasure the days we
> may go. Generally in the afternoon we drive to one
> of the woods and lay in our hammocks there. Our
> old Sandy is very well and happy, but we cannot
> take him out with us as he barks so fearfully. We
> have got a very nice lawn where we play croquet in
> the garden belonging to the house where Uncle
> Phillip* lives when he is here, it is a very nice
> place as it is so near to our house, and the garden
> is very shady so that we can play even though it is
> very hot and sunny.[15]

*Prince Philip of Saxe-Coburg Kohary, elder brother of Ferdinand, Prince of Bulgaria.

Visits to the theatre were a special treat, and in a letter the following year (21 May 1890), Ducky described excitedly how they were 'rejoycing [sic] very much at the idea of the little trip we are going to make to Oberammergau to see the "Passionspiel".'[16]

In the winter they enjoyed skating, and in November 1891 helped with a charity bazaar, which Ducky wrote about enthusiastically to the Queen (27 November 1891): 'It has been a great success, above all expectations. It was a very pretty sight; all the young ladies who sold in the stalls were costumed as different peasants and the stalls themselves were like little houses and were beautifully decorated.'[17]

Yet there were two baneful influences on their young lives at this point. One was an arrogant, tyrannical man, Alfred's tutor, who won the Duchess's favour by means of his great erudition. He hated everything that was English, and he had the Duchess's full approval in his attempts to uproot his young charges' love of England and turning them into good patriotic Germans. As he was such an unpleasant character, his methods had the opposite effect. The princesses especially resented his tyrannical treatment of their brother, ridiculing him in front of others and destroying such self-confidence as he might have possessed. In her memoirs, Missy could only bring herself to refer to this objectionable character as 'Dr X'.

Their other *bête noire*, referred to cryptically as 'Fraulein', was their governess. She was something of a wolf in sheep's clothing. Outwardly charming, friendly, and the kind of person who encouraged the girls to confide in her, her apparent good nature belied the influence she wielded over the household. As far as the Duchess was concerned, it was only Fraulein's advice or opinions which ever counted. Any servant who displeased her in any way would be instantly dismissed, any friendship between the Duchess or her daughters which was 'not approved of,' would be systematically undermined. Like Dr X, she helped see to it that the girls were brought up with German manners, tastes and ideas. She persuaded the Duchess that it would be good to counter any possible vanity in her daughters by forcing them to wear ugly clothes, harsh linen and coarse calico. Humiliatingly ugly gowns, hats and cloaks, and badly-shaped shoes, all in drab colours, would likewise help to extinguish any tendency towards self-indulgence. She had a hateful way of showing the princesses up to their mother in a most unattractive light. Moreover, she encouraged and stimulated petty jealousies among the girls, and only a genuine bond of filial love kept them united throughout the years at Coburg.

Life in the German duchy was much less agreeable when the Duchess was away. The unprepossessing tutor and governess duly fell in love and became engaged, and thus united, were a formidable force *in loco parentis* towards their three charges. (Baby Bee, much younger, was rarely parted from her mother at this time.) However, in the rebellious Ducky, they met their match one day.

A large silver cup, filled with flowers or a plant, always stood in the centre of the dining table. When the Duchess was away, Fraulein sat at the head, and Dr X at the foot. Naturally this cup prevented the adoring couple from gazing fondly into each other's eyes at meals. They put up with this obstacle for some time, until Dr X highhandedly ordered a servant to take it away. The girls immediately protested; Mama had placed it there, she alone had the right to order its removal, and as they were her children they could not allow it to be touched. Dr X tried to laugh away their childish objections, but they would not give way. Exasperated, he exclaimed contemptuously, 'Well, it is either I or the pot!' At this, Ducky stretched out her arms, clasped the cup to her chest, and glared at him. 'We prefer the pot!' she shouted. With as much dignity as he could muster, the defeated tutor left the table. Those who were left passed the meal in icy silence, but the admiring Missy and Sandra were secretly proud and delighted that Ducky had stood her ground so successfully.[18]

As Missy had perceptively said:

Sister Ducky was more austere, more unbending
than I was. She was always the monitor; the one
who would tolerate no nonsense, who admonished
or cautioned. Her advice or reproof was listened to
and there was a steel-like rectitude about her
which commanded respect.[19]

Not everybody at Coburg from the elder generation was so disliked, however. Ducky and Missy had made great friends with Meister, the Rosenau castellan. Ugly, unshaven and slightly crippled, he was an irrepressible eccentric beloved by all the family. He was forever inventing and discovering things, and had a perpetual fund of stories, all calculated to appeal to an adolescent's imagination. He helped the two elder princesses to build a small hut out of an old cupboard in the Rosenau thickets. It was roomy, worm-eaten, and rather decrepit, but over it he added a gable, and on the outside he fixed up a bell with a horseshoe for good luck hanging from its rope. Ducky and Missy lovingly painted it grass-green, with a large red heart on the door. The red paint ran as they did so, and so in order to relieve the solemnity of this bleeding heart, they added small bunches of daisies and a border of four-leaved clovers. Naturally the hut was very small, with no room for a fireplace. A tree branch passed through it; from this they suspended a miniature cauldron, hung by a thick, heavily-rusted chain, and filled it with flowers.

In August 1890 the Duke of Edinburgh took up his post as Commander-in-Chief at Devonport, an appointment which was to last for nearly three years. His wife and daughters spent little time in Devon with him, though after a family Christmas at Coburg that year the Duchess joined him shortly after his return to port. Although she was persuaded to put in occasional appearances, she much preferred her independence in Coburg, and did not relish the role of a Commander-in-Chief's wife in England.

By now, in fact she no longer relished her position as his wife at all. Four years later, she wrote with some bitterness to her (by then married) eldest daughter that, throughout her married life, she had felt like no more than her husband's 'legitimate mistress'.[20]

The princesses only came to Devon during vacations, but they enjoyed the experience more than their mother. Missy spoke for all of them when she eulogized over 'that beautiful county of Devonshire, so enchanting with its hills and dales, its rivers and forests, its steep roads and high hedges, beautiful gardens and, in places, quite southern vegetation.'[21] Their official residence, Admiralty House, was uninteresting and notable only for a minute rear garden where they indulged in quarrelsome games of croquet. More enticing were the house and garden of the General-in-Command opposite, Sir Richard Harrison, and his family. Their daughters were the same age as the princesses, and all became close friends, inseparable in their games and swimming expeditions.

A contemporary Plymouth observer, Hilda Picken, recalled many years later what it was like to have royalty in their midst. The Duchess, she commented,

> obviously felt she had come down in the social
> scale, having married a mere Duke, and being
> obliged to come into contact with the likes of us.

All their pretty daughters were at home and
unmarried, and apparently found life in a Service
town a very cheerful affair. The contrast between
their gay young faces and Mama's glowering looks
was quite remarkable.[22]

Inevitably, the minds of the elder generation were turning
towards choosing husbands for the Edinburgh princesses.
The Duchess of Edinburgh had a theory that princesses
should marry young; once they reached the age of twenty,
they began to think too much and to have too many ideas
of their own, besides which an unmarried princess 'had
no position at all'.

Had the Duchess not intervened, Missy would have
almost certainly gone to the altar as bride of her cousin
Prince George of Wales. Queen Victoria and the Duke of
Edinburgh thoroughly approved of the idea, but once the
Duchess realized, she ordered her daughter to write
'cousin Georgie' a stiffly-worded note to the effect that he
must not think there was anything definite in the
friendship that had formed between them in Malta.
Although she liked her nephew, she was adamant that no
daughter of hers would marry an English prince. With
almost indecent haste, she took Missy to Germany, where
she was introduced to the well-meaning but ineffectual
Crown Prince Ferdinand ('Nando'). He had been informed
through the Duchess that Princess Marie was 'available',
and in the fashion of the time, requested her photograph
before their meeting. Knowing that her cousin Prince
George also had hopes of marrying her, he knew he had to
act quickly. His parents were as determined as he and the
Duchess were, and almost before she realized what was
happening, Missy was betrothed.

It was only to be expected, therefore, that the question
of a husband for Ducky would be settled before long. By

the time her father relinquished his command at Devon-port, in June 1893, she was aged sixteen, and the match-making process had begun in earnest.

CHAPTER *3*

'Very charming and distinguée'

*W*hen it came to the question of marriages for her descendants, Queen Victoria generally had firm ideas on the subject. She had a particular place in her heart for her motherless Hesse grandchildren, her second daughter Alice having succumbed to diphtheria in December 1878 at the early age of thirty-five, leaving a widower, four daughters, and one surviving son. The latter, Ernest ('Ernie'), was good-looking, somewhat excitable, way-ward and very high-spirited. He had inherited little of the militarism of his father and grandfather, and had more enthusiasm for the arts. He drew and painted well, encouraged theatre at Darmstadt, was fond of pranks and practical jokes, and inclined to be casual about answering letters.

In the autumn of 1891, Ernie and Ducky were both among Queen Victoria's guests at Balmoral. Ernie, in his customary high spirits, appeared to be quite taken with his tall, dark-haired Edinburgh cousin. They shared the same birthday (Ernie being the elder by eight years) and a similar sense of humour, and seemed to rush about in a private world of their own. Their grandmother told Ernie's eldest sister, Princess Louis of Battenberg, that they were 'very funny together'.[1]

The princess knew instantly what the Queen was thinking. A perceptive, responsible young woman, she had virtually taken her mother's place in helping to bring up her brother and younger sisters. She had her doubts on the wisdom of such a marriage, on grounds of character. Ernie and Ducky were superficially very lively characters, and similar in many ways – too similar, in fact, for comfort. He had been grossly spoilt since losing his mother, and was used to having his own way. She had a reputation for being determined and headstrong. Would their personalities clash? Where their inheritance was concerned, Grand Duke Louis's health was failing, and it was likely that his son would succeed him before long. Princess Louis wondered whether they would be responsible or mature enough to shoulder the duties of a Grand Duke and Duchess of Hesse and the Rhine.

Other misgivings were expressed about the health risks of such an alliance. Ernie's brother Frederick ('Frittie'), a haemophiliac, had bled to death after a fall at the age of two and a half. Although Ernie himself was not haemophiliac, it was feared (wrongly) that Ducky might be a carrier of the disease. Admittedly she was much more robust than her Wales cousins (of whom the youngest, Maud, had been briefly considered as a possible bride for him), but the risk of marriages between first cousins descended from Queen Victoria was deemed too great.

Mindful of such considerations, the Queen spoke to her doctor, Sir William Jenner. A few weeks after Grand Duke Louis died in March 1892 and Ernie's succession to the Grand Duchy made the question of his marriage more urgent than ever, she reported to Princess Louis that Jenner said there could be no possible danger in Ernie marrying one of his Edinburgh cousins. They were all so strong and healthy, as was their mother, and that 'if the relations were strong intermarriage with them only led to greater strength & health.' Shortly before his death, Grand Duke Louis had also expressed a wish that his son should marry Ducky.

What really hardened Queen Victoria's resolve to see

the match go ahead, however, was the sudden engagement of Missy to Crown Prince Ferdinand. She professed herself 'much startled' by the news, not to say dismayed. Although he was 'nice' and his parents 'charming', marriage into such an insecure country as Roumania, and society's immorality at Bucharest, made the prospect much less appealing. The Prince of Wales had believed that Missy was going to be betrothed to George, still recovering from a severe attack of typhoid the previous year and in a thoroughly fragile state after the death of his elder brother 'Eddy', Duke of Clarence, from influenza. Although the brothers had usually been on the best of terms, the Prince of Wales angrily accused the Duke of Edinburgh of snubbing his son. It was an unfair accusation as the Duke, too, had fervently hoped for such a match, and held much the same views as Queen Victoria regarding an Anglo-Roumanian marriage. As Queen Victoria had said, it was 'the dream of Affie's life' to see his nephew Prince George become his son-in-law as well. For a while family relationships were considerably strained.

Missy's engagement and marriage to Ferdinand in January 1893 made no difference to the close affinity between her and Ducky. 'I certainly will miss Missy dreadfully and the time when we are to lose her is approaching fast,' Ducky wrote sadly from Admiralty House to Queen Victoria (26 November 1892). 'But we try not to think too much about it so as not to sadden the last few weeks which we will spend together.'[2] Yet her elder sister's departure cast a cloud over the seasonal celebrations the following month; 'We have spent such a happy Christmas for the last time together with Missy,'[3] was the mournful refrain (26 December 1892).

It was typical of their mother's tactlessness that she instructed Ducky to write Missy lively letters about her court balls, her new friends, and other activities. The

Duchess mistakenly hoped that Missy would be cheered to hear what a happy time her sister was having. But the real effect was to make the homesick Crown Princess of Roumania more miserable still at the knowledge of what she was missing, and afraid that others had usurped her place in her beloved sister's affections. This was certainly not the case. Ducky was pining just as much on her part, and she was taken to stay at St Petersburg 'to help her over the parting which she had minded almost tragically, for her nature was deep and loving and always somewhat stormy.'[4]

Thwarted in their plans for the eldest daughter, Queen Victoria and the Duke of Edinburgh were determined to have their way over the second.

As for the young couple, they were unenthusiastic. Like Missy and George, they were 'beloved chums', and enjoyed each other's company, but only up to a point. Just because they were first cousins and had had one particularly cheerful holiday together did not make it a foregone conclusion that they would be ideally suited as husband and wife. In particular Ernie was not attracted to her; he preferred male company. However, if Queen Victoria ardently wished such a match to take place, he would never dream of not acquiescing. A letter he wrote her (15 March 1893) on the first anniversary of his father's death reveals something of the close bond between him and his grandmother:

Please forgive me for not writing any sooner, but the anniversary of all those awfull [sic] days made us all so unhappy that it was all I could do to keep sisters safe from breaking down. I still cannot believe that it is allready [sic] a year since all this sorrow came to us. But one thing I must say darling Grandmama that if it had not been for the great love you showed us in all this time I do not

know how we would have got over it, & my one
prayer is that you will keep it for us as you have
done all these years since darling Mama died, for
you have always been a second mother to me. That
is the reason why we will all our lives never be able
to thank you enough for all you have done to
us . . .[5]

The Duchess of Edinburgh, needless to say, hoped that
a Romanov husband would be found for her second
daughter. Although there were several bachelor Grand
Dukes in Russia about her age, the Russian Orthodox
Church forbade marriages between first cousins. As the
union of Queen Victoria and Prince Albert in 1840 had
made manifestly clear, the Protestant Church had no
such rule.

In August 1893, the Duke of Coburg caught a chill
while out hunting, and died a few days later, aged
seventy-five. The Duke of Edinburgh's naval career had
come to an end two months previously, with the expiry of
his command at Devonport and his elevation in rank to
Admiral of the Fleet. That his uncle should have died so
soon afterwards was convenient from one point of view,
but Affie did not take up his inheritance with any great
enthusiasm. He had loved naval service; to take up his
duties in a small German Duchy was not an appealing
prospect, even though he had been prepared for it from
an early age.

But first there was the matter of his second daughter's
betrothal to settle. That autumn, Missy in Roumania was
due to give birth to her first child. While the Duchess of
Edinburgh went to be with her, the Duke took advantage
of his wife's absence to further the matchmaking process
with Queen Victoria. Between them, they dismissed such
opposition to their plans as still existed. In her own
words, the Queen 'had it out' with the Duchess on her

return from Roumania, and wrote repeatedly to Ernie 'about the *necessity* of his showing some attention and interest'. George, she told him, had 'lost Missy by waiting and waiting'.[6]

Despite any misgivings he felt about marriage and fatherhood in general, and Ducky in particular, Ernie was anxious to reassure the Queen (6 October 1893) that:

> I have not changed the very least & I beg you to
> let Aunt M. know that I feel just the same as I
> have done all the time & only for Ducky's sake I
> had not gone to Coburg because I did not want the
> people to begin talking about her. When she is
> back I will try to go & see them . . .[7]

Two months later, the issue was as good as settled. Ernie wrote to the Queen (18 December 1893):

> I have just returned yesterday from Coburg, where
> I spent very happy days. I have very good news to
> tell you, my prospects are very good? Ducky has
> been all these days so dear and so kind to me that
> I have got the very best hopes. I am certain that if
> I wanted to ask her now she would say yes. But I
> did not because I wanted to tell it to you first. The
> situations between Uncle Alfred and me now are
> so changed since I talked to you last year in
> England that I want to ask you again about our
> marriage. Uncle is now a German Prince & is
> doing everything so wonderfully well that all his
> subjects are simply devoted to him. I heard all this
> now when I was there. He has shown so much love
> & tact that the people simply addore [sic] him. I
> am afraid that for this reason now that the idea of
> having my wedding in England will be impossible.
> For it would harm him so much, he would hurt his

people & dissapoint [sic] them at the same time &
it would make me miserable to think that I was the
cause of bringing him into trouble. I have also
asked different people here . . . & they all said the
same that if the wedding was in England it would
harm him very much & the people here would say
about me that I ought to have been sensible &
stopped it.[8]

Events took their course, and on 9 January 1894 the
Duke of Coburg delightedly wired his mother: 'Your and
my great wish has been fulfilled this evening. Ducky has
accepted Ernie of Hesse's proposal. We are a very happy
family party.'[9]

Ducky added, in a letter to the Queen (18 January
1894):

You will forgive my not having written to you yet
I am sure as the last few days we had scarcely time
for anything. I need not tell you how happy I am,
I know how fond you are of dear Ernie and you can
easily imagine it. It is also so delightful that
Darmstadt is so near, it will not seem like leaving
home so entirely. We spent such a happy time
now all together. It was so nice that Alix came too.
I think she enjoyed being here; we had a ball
whilst she was here and she danced very much and
was very gay. They also have a great deal going on
at Darmstadt and had to leave so soon that all
that happened in that short time seems still like a
dream to me. It was so nice that Missy was
also just here and so we were all together
but unhappily they too had to leave so soon as
they wished to stay still a short time at
Sigmaringen.[10]

From Berlin, the Empress Frederick greeted the news with joy, tempered only by her reservations about the close relationship:

> If only she were not his 1st cousin, what could be
> nicer? She is a charming girl, bright and clever,
> with plenty of spirit, which is rather what he
> wants, and then it is so nice to think that it will
> not be a stranger in dear Alice's place.[11]

The Duchess of Edinburgh reacted with predictably bad grace. Shortly after the betrothal was announced, she had a long and private conversation with Ernie about his grandmother and what she contemptuously called 'the English family', and 'why we could not really like them and how often they had been nasty and spiteful to me,' as she told Missy. 'He must not always be dragging Ducky to England in perpetual adoration of Granny and . . . (he must) understand the reasons why *we* can *never* adore her.'[12]

Ironically, in view of what was to happen, at the time this marriage was regarded as the best, in dynastic terms, of all the Edinburgh marriages. Some journalists in European capitals, notably one on the Viennese *Neues Wiener Tagblatt,* invested it with a political significance that must have seemed a little far-fetched, even by the standards of the time:

> The conclusion of the Russo-German commercial
> treaty gave a friendly turn to the relations between
> Russia and Germany, while those between Russia
> and Austria-Hungary have long been of a
> satisfactory character. These improved relations
> between the Powers included in the Triple Alliance
> and Russia have everywhere cleared the political
> horizon. The wedding at Coburg and the presence

there of the Cesarewitch are symptomatic of this,
and it may be that personal intercourse between
the Emperor William and the Russian Heir-
Apparent will still further advance the *rapprochement*
between the two States. The House of Coburg has
already given the country Princes devoted to peace.
Whether the sons of that House have obtained
positions of high influence in London, Brussels, or
Lisbon they have everywhere exerted themselves in
the interests of peace, a task which has been
greatly facilitated by their connexions with most of
the ruling families . . . Without going too far in the
way of political speculation, it is evident that the
Coburg wedding is a striking symptom of peace.[13]

The wedding was to be celebrated with festivities such as
Coburg had not seen for many years. As Ernie's letter had
made clear as tactfully as possible, now that the bride's
father was Duke of Coburg, it would have been impolitic
to offend German sensibilities by having the ceremony in
England. However, as Queen Victoria would have to
travel there to attend, the time of year was arranged to
suit her as far as possible. Late April or early May would
be the latest dates feasible; if it was postponed till the
summer, the heat would be too much for her.

Thus in the third week of April 1894, guests made their
way into the normally sleepy little German duchy. They
made up the greatest throng of royalty to be seen together
at one place since the gathering for Queen Victoria's
jubilee in 1887. They included Queen Victoria and most
of her surviving children, Emperor William and his
brother Prince Henry, the bride's brother and sisters
(including Missy, who was expecting her second child),
the bridegroom's sisters, and three representatives of
imperial Russia who were destined to play important,

very differing roles in Ducky's later life – the Tsarevich, and his uncle and aunt, Grand Duke and Duchess Vladimir. All attended a family dinner hosted by the Duke and Duchess, and a gala performance at the Riesensaal on the eve of the wedding. Among the other celebrations were torchlight processions, and an amnesty in which the Duke pardoned prisoners convicted of minor offences.

On the morning of 19 April, thousands of people streamed into the Schlossplatz to see as many visiting royalty as possible. They must have been disappointed, for the chapel was an integral part of the Schloss, and there was no public procession outside the building.

The chapel had been decorated in most picturesque fashion. There were festoons of garlands made from fir twigs, hung from pillar to pillar, wound around the marble columns flanking the pulpit, which was covered with white flowers.

At 11.00 in the morning, a short civil marriage cere-mony was performed privately in the Queen's apartments. Soon afterwards, the company began to assemble in the chapel. At 11.50 the band stationed in the courtyard struck up the German national anthem, thus announcing the approach of the royal procession. One of the least conspicuous guests of all, the Dowager Duchess of Coburg in her widow's weeds, took up her position in a small private gallery at the lower end of the chapel, with six ladies-in-waiting.

Soon after midday Prince von Ratibor, Grand Marshal of the Court, attended by other marshals and officials, appeared at the chapel entrance and gave three taps on the floor with his wand of office. This signified the entrance of the procession of guests. First was the German Emperor, attired proudly in the uniform of a Hessian general, leading the Duchess of Coburg. Next came the Empress Frederick, alone, followed by the Prince of Wales, in his First Dragoon of Guards uniform, walking next to the Tsarevich, in the uniform of a Hussar of the Russian Guard. Behind them was a long train of princes and princesses. After they had taken up their positions, Ratibor came to announce the approach of bridegroom and best man, his uncle Prince William of Hesse. The groom arrived, resplendent in the same general's uniform as the Emperor, with helmet and red and white plumes. After a pause, the entrance of Queen Victoria was announced, as she came into sight leaning on the arm of the Duke of Coburg, who conducted her to a gilded chair in the centre of the first row of seats. Then came the bride and her maids, her sister Beatrice and Princess Feodora of Saxe-Meiningen.

The service opened with the singing of an anthem, followed by an address from Muller, the officiating court chaplain. As he read the service, rings were exchanged. Then, said *The Times*, 'the venerable Court Chaplain, who was deeply moved, invoked a blessing upon the young couple in a voice broken with emotion',[14] followed by the Lord's Prayer, and a Benediction.

The wedding breakfast took place in the Throne Room. Afterwards, the crowds who had been waiting ever since early in the morning thronged to see the couple drive off from the Schlossplatz, in a phaeton decorated liberally with spring flowers. As members of the party escorted the young couple to their carriage, there were affectionate leave-takings all round, and handfuls of rice were thrown over the steps, the foremost in observing this traditional custom being the Emperor William, the Prince of Wales and Duke of Connaught. They drove off amid hearty *'Hochs!'*. While the guests waved them goodbye, four enterprising photographers ran into the courtyard square and frantically signalled to the assembled company not to move. Far from regarding this as an intrusion on their dignity, the most distinguished gathering to be seen anywhere in Europe that year, smiling good-naturedly, posed for several photographs. They were just in time, for a few minutes later sunshine gave way to such violent thunderstorms that the town's evening illuminations had to be postponed.

After the wedding, Ernie and Ducky made their state entry into Darmstadt. Bands played, church bells pealed, the town was gaily bedecked with flags, and the streets were filled with happy, cheering crowds. In an open carriage, filled to overflowing with bunches of roses, irises and lilacs, the Grand Duchess, looking very slim, in a pale mauve dress and a flowered toque, raised her head in answer to her husband's gesture as she smiled and waved.

The Empress Frederick described the wedding in a letter to her daughter Sophie, Crown Princess of the Hellenes, who had been unable to attend:

> Ducky looked very charming and *distinguée*. She had a plain white silk gown with hardly any trimming, and Aunt Alice's wedding veil, a light slender diadem of emeralds with a sprig of orange blossom stuck in behind. It all suited her charmingly. During the service Aunt Marie was very calm, but the tears rolled down Uncle Alfred's cheeks, and Grandmama's and mine too . . . [15]

Apparently there were other reasons than emotional ones for the Queen's tears. Behind the scenes, there had been much family dismay at her ardent championship of 'the Munshi', her privileged Indian servant, Abdul Karim. The Munshi's arrogance had given him ideas above his station very soon after he had been taken into royal employment, and he was included in the suite that accompanied Queen Victoria to Coburg for the wedding. The Duke of Coburg had asked his equerry to tell the Queen's secretary, Sir Henry Ponsonby, that nothing would induce him to allow the Munshi into the chapel for the wedding, ostensibly on religious grounds. The Queen was furious, and after much argument it was arranged by way of compromise that the Munshi could watch from a gallery in the church. On being escorted there, he was apparently content until he saw he was sitting with some of the grooms. Angrily, he got up and left the church without staying for the service, and afterwards he wrote the Queen an indignant letter complaining of this high-handed treatment. She was bitterly upset.

Another close relation who was disturbed at the marriage, although for very different reasons, was the groom's youngest sister, Princess Alix. Ever since her father's death, the pathologically shy 'Alicky' had acted as hostess – albeit a very timid, self-effacing one – at the court of her bachelor brother. Apart from a determined, autocratic streak, she had nothing in common with the self-assured cousin who was now marrying this brother.

According to Princess Catherine Radziwill, when Alicky received her telegram in January announcing her brother's betrothal, she was so angry that only with difficulty could she be persuaded by her ladies-in-waiting to send her congratulations to the couple. She hated the idea of having a sister-in-law to take her place, which she had imagined would be hers until she herself married. It was alleged that she caused a stormy scene with her brother, only to be told firmly by him that his marriage was none of her business, and if she no longer wished to live at Darmstadt then she was free to take herself off to one of his shooting-boxes with her own lady-in-waiting. She bowed to the inevitable, and wrote Ducky a note of congratulation in the end, but by the time of the wedding she was in a sullen frame of mind.

Princess Radziwill was a notorious gossip, and one must suspect a degree of imagination in her report of a blazing quarrel between brother and sister who had always been so devoted. Nonetheless, it was common knowledge that the news had not been sweet music to Alicky's ears.

She did not relish playing second fiddle to Ducky and her domineering mother. For some time it had been common knowledge throughout the courts of Europe that Alicky had been deeply devoted to Tsarevich Nicholas, yet reluctant to embrace the Russian Orthodox Church. This, and a little persuasion from Emperor William who knew that the young lovers needed some gentle encouragement, helped her to make up her mind. On the morning after the wedding, it was confirmed that Alicky and Nicky were betrothed.

For a while, it looked as if the marriage of the Grand Duke of Hesse and his Edinburgh cousin would be the happy union which most of the family had expected or hoped it would be. Ernie and Ducky were as wayward and irresponsible as Queen Victoria had feared they would be. Many were the complaints to Princess Louis of Battenberg, whom she still expected to keep a firm maternal eye on her younger brother, that they would not answer letters or telegrams.

CHAPTER 4

'A period of magnificent enjoyment'

*W*ithin a few months, the Grand Duchess of Hesse was expecting a child. She was therefore unable to accompany her husband to Russia for the Tsar's wedding later that year. In view of the antipathy between Ducky and the new Tsarina, perhaps it was just as well.

The Empress Frederick visited Ducky and found her looking 'lovely, but very pale, and her figure showing scarcely anything of impending events. She is such a dear and so sympathetic, unaffected, gentle and ladylike.'[1]

On 11 March 1895 she gave birth to a daughter, who was named Elizabeth. All the family were delighted, especially the proud father. Queen Victoria hoped that parenthood would now induce the couple to settle down, and that soon they would present the grand duchy with a male heir.

Only those closest to them could see how unsuited they were to each other. They had had little chance to get to know each other during their engagement. Once married, they behaved more like brother and sister than husband and wife. While in the company of others, life was one never-ending party. Just as the Prince and Princess of Wales had brought a long-vanished gaiety to society life in London shortly after their marriage in 1863, so did the Grand Duke and his vivacious wife to the quiet little German territory – for a while.

It seemed to observers as if they both lived solely for

pleasure. Friends and relations were invited to the most informal of house parties at Wolfsgarten, where titles gave way to nicknames, and everyone behaved as they wished. They sat on the floor, painted, rode their horses, or jousted on bicycles in the woods. Instead of signing a visitors' book, they scratched their names on a window-pane in the main salon. Prince Nicholas of Greece called his stay at Wolfsgarten 'the jolliest, merriest house party to which I have ever been in my life', and likened the general atmosphere to that of 'schoolchildren on a holiday'.[2]

Royal children, used to stern discipline at home and at other courts, revelled in the freedom they were allowed at Darmstadt. Ernie and Ducky had built a miniature play-house for Elizabeth, and her young cousins enjoyed many a rough-and-tumble between its walls. Adults were for-bidden to enter, much to the frustration of royal nurses and tutors, who could be seen pacing up and down impatiently outside as they waited for their high-spirited young charges to stop their games and emerge.

Among the closest friends of the Grand Duke and Duchess were the British Ambassador to Hesse and his wife, Sir George and Lady Buchanan. Being some years older than their hosts, they were treated with the greatest respect, and provided a ready shoulder for both to lean on.

This did not, however, spare them from becoming the butt of royal pranks. In the woods there was a small pond, full of mud, covered with duckweed and surrounded by bullrushes. On one side was a steep slope, down which Ernie had constructed a water chute. It was used mostly by the men, who would ride down it in a small boat, even though they were usually drenched by a muddy spray from the pond by the time it hit the water. One day Ernie and Nicholas of Greece persuaded Lady Buchanan and one of the ladies-in-waiting to go with them, having arranged beforehand to upset the boat deliberately. Lady Buchanan had put on a new pink dress of which she was very proud. Needless to say, it proved unequal to virtual immersion in the pond. She crawled out wet and dirty, and the dress shrank so much after being washed that it was only fit for her small (and delighted) daughter Meriel.

Another day, when everybody was sitting in the courtyard after lunch, a servant handing out coffee was startled to see two peasant women in checked aprons, coloured handkerchiefs over their heads, coming in through the open gates that led into the woods. He walked over at once to tell them tactfully that they were trespassing on private property, and then almost dropped his tray in astonishment as he recognized the Grand Duchess and Lady Buchanan, both helpless with laughter.

Ernie and Ducky throve on the distractions of such amusements, and loved – even needed – plenty of company around them. When left to themselves, it was a different story. For Ducky, like her mother, was used to doing things her own way. Just as the Duchess of Edinburgh had found fault with almost everything about her in-laws' court and way of life, so did the Grand Duchess of Hesse quickly lose patience with the traditions of her husband's domains. Her predecessor Alice had gently risen above anti-English prejudice after marrying Prince Louis of Hesse in 1862, by recognizing the value of proceeding cautiously when she wanted to introduce ideas of her own. In doing so, she went a long way towards gaining the people's love and respect.

Ducky was impatient with such ideas. She had nothing but contempt for the unwritten rules and regulations governing the life of *Die Landesmutter* (Mother of the Land). She resented giving up her time to perform duties expected of her; she forgot, or did not bother, to answer letters; and she postponed, or else avoided, paying visits to relations whom she did not like. At official receptions she caused needless offence by talking to people who amused her, and thereby ignoring dignitaries whose local standing entitled them to a greater call on her time.

Such behaviour inevitably led to friction with her husband. Much as he enjoyed their parties and pranks together, he appreciated that his position entailed a sense of responsibility. He had been well schooled by his father and by Queen Victoria, and he respected the legacy of his mother whose health had in part been sacrificed to shouldering burdens beyond the call of duty. That his wife should baulk at making at least an effort to do the same was tantamount to insulting her memory. His reproaches led to displays of her ungovernable temper, and many a tea table laden with china came off worst in the process.

The differences in their characters became apparent all too soon. There was more to Ernie than the fun-loving extrovert. This mask hid the personality of a highly-strung young man who had never really got over the shock of losing a younger brother, a younger sister, and soon afterwards a mother, during his first eleven years. Sometimes all he wanted was to be left on his own. If he chose to lie in bed on a fine summer's day writing mournful poetry, he did so. To him, horses were a means of transport, but the idea of using them merely for recreation made him nervous.

The fearless Ducky adored horses. Animals were sent from England, Russia and Vienna to her stables at Wolfsgarten. When she preferred her own company she would go into the woods, sometimes on horseback, sometimes in a carriage four-in-hand, or even six-in-hand, driving through the trees and along dusty roads at a reckless pace which made others fear for her safety. If she came back two hours later and found that she had missed or forgotten an important engagement, what did it matter? Any reproach from her husband would bring forth angry accusations of cowardice or laziness because he had not accompanied her.

Her favourite horse, a fiery black stallion named Bogdan, had come from the Russian steppes. His temper matched hers, and she was the only person he would obey. In her more wilful moods it amused her to let him loose in the courtyard, chasing terrified servants, helping himself to the contents of the flower beds, or feasting wickedly from the decorations on hats of any ladies careless enough to be around. One day he took the seat out of the Grand Duke's trousers as he fled for safety. Ducky's laughter ringing out across the courtyard at this undignified sight did not further the cause of marital bliss.

Ducky had her champions, mostly among the German relations, who considered that she would doubtless grow up in time. The Empress Frederick had nothing but praise for her, describing her to Sophie of the Hellenes, after a visit to Hesse (August 1895), as 'looking so handsome, and having her hair gathered off the forehead and put up in natural waves and a loose twist behind suits her wonderfully and shows up her pretty white young brow.'[3]

In spring again the following year, the Empress noted that Heinrich von Angeli was at Darmstadt painting her portrait; 'I envy him, she is so handsome that it must be a real pleasure. I admire her still more than her sisters-in-law, Ella and Alicky, lovely though they are.'[4]

Ducky enjoyed being at the court of Berlin. The large scale and colourful pageantry of Prussian court life impressed her more favourably than the comparative dullness of England, and the formality of Darmstadt, when there were no guests or house parties to liven things up. She liked and was admired by the Empress Augusta

The wedding of the Duke and Duchess of
Edinburgh at St Petersburg, Russian
Orthodox Ceremony, 23 January 1874

Prince Alfred as midshipman, *c*.1858

Alexander II, Tsar of Russia, and Grand
Duchess Marie

Marie, Duchess of Edinburgh, 1875

The daughters of the Duke and Duchess of Edinburgh, June 1888. *From left*: Princess Marie; Princess Beatrice (*in front*); Princess Victoria Melita; Princess Alexandra

Above The Grand Duke and Duchess of
Hesse and the Rhine on their wedding day,
19 April 1894
Above right Shooting expedition at Coburg,
*c.*1896. *From left*: Prince Alfred; Nicholas II,
Tsar of Russia; the Grand Duke of Hesse
and the Rhine; the Duke of Saxe-Coburg
Gotha

Right The Grand Duchess of Hesse and the
Rhine, after a painting by *Heinrich von Angeli*,
1896

The Duchess of Saxe-Coburg Gotha (*far left*) and her three elder daughters, 1898. *From left*: Marie, Crown Princess of Roumania; the Grand Duchess of Hesse and the Rhine; Princess Ernest of Hohenlohe-Langenburg

The Grand Duchess of Hesse and the Rhine, *c*. 1896

The Grand Duke of Hesse

The Duke of Saxe-Coburg Gotha, 1900

Grand Duke Cyril in uniform of the
Imperial Guards Marines

Grand Duchess Cyril of Russia (*on left*) and her sisters, 1905. *From left*:
Marie, Crown Princess of Roumania; Princess Ernest of
Hohenlohe-Langenburg; Princess Beatrice of Saxe-Coburg Gotha

Alexandra, Tsarina of Russia

Princess Ernest of Hohenlohe-Langenburg

Marie, Crown Princess of Roumania

Grand Duchess Cyril of Russia

Victoria ('Dona'), and her discontent at home was probably due in part to the warm reception she was always accorded at the German capital.

Ducky and Dona shared a love of horses, and would ride together at military parades, their appearances presenting an unintentionally comic contrast. Ducky's slim, dignified figure showed up the unprepossessing demeanour of her plain, fat cousin, whose bearing on horseback was described by her contemporaries as being more like a sack of potatoes in the saddle.

Ducky found a ready refuge with the Empress, who had great sympathy for her in her marriage difficulties. The Empress disliked her English in-laws, and resented the matriarchal domination Queen Victoria exercised over her family throughout Europe. In due course this influence made itself felt on Ducky, eighteen years her junior, reinforcing the anti-English prejudices which her mother had tried to instil in her, albeit with limited success. This influence also contributed to chilly relations between the courts of St Petersburg and Berlin. The Tsarina, who had always worshipped Grandmama at Windsor, grew to dislike Ducky more and more, and inevitably she took the side of her brother whom she felt was being slighted.

Ducky and Missy were overjoyed when they met again for a month's holiday on the Isle of Wight in the summer of 1895. The Crown Princess of Roumania had her children, Carol, aged eighteen months, and baby Elisabetha. The Grand Duchess of Hesse had brought her Elizabeth, also a babe in arms, and all shared a cottage lent by Queen Victoria. The youthful sisters – neither had yet celebrated their twentieth birthdays – relished being back in the cherished haunts of their childhood. Once more they were at liberty to explore the beach with its shells, watch the coastguards at work, and walk alongside the slippery pier with its multicoloured seaweed.

Their chief mode of transport was a small one-horse pony trap which they drove in turns as far as the ferry to Cowes. Here they browsed happily in gift shops, looking for presents to give the sailors who had become the children's willing slaves as readily as they had once been theirs.

There was something homely about 'Grandmama Queen', less intimidating now than when they were small, as she sat in the garden for breakfast under her green-lined parasol, surrounded by Indian and Highland servants, and trained dogs. Away from Anglophobe influences at foreign courts, and in the company of her more easy-going sister, Ducky could once again appreciate the virtues of living in England.

The sisters were together again a year later, as guests at the coronation of the Tsar and Tsarina. It was a family reunion of sorts, for not only were the sisters and their husbands present, but also their parents and brother Alfred. This last Romanov coronation was sadly destined to be remembered less for the splendour of the ceremonies themselves, than for the horror of Khodinsky Meadow, at which a free open-air feast for the citizens of Moscow turned into a mass stampede of drunken spectators jostling for souvenir gifts and food, with an estimated two thousand crushed to death in the resulting panic.

For Ducky and Missy, however, the coronation and its attendant festivities provided an opportunity to indulge themselves in dressing up in fine clothes and jewels, while experiencing to some degree the court life which they had never known before marriage and had so far been denied the opportunity to savour at the courts of Hesse and Roumania. The Duchess of Edinburgh thoroughly disapproved, reluctant to believe that her two elder daughters were now wives and mothers themselves, with minds of their own. Missy recorded in her memoirs that:

> Her withering criticism of the way we wore our
> veils under diadems, which she considered too
> picturesque and not orthodox enough, still makes
> my cheeks burn . . . (she) deplored our tendency
> towards picturesque 'affectation', and when we
> knew she would be present, we had to refrain from
> too much artistic imagination.[5]

Fortunately they found a ready ally in Grand Duchess Alexandra, Great-aunt 'Sari', widow of Grand Duke Constantine, brother of Tsar Alexander II. Hearing her niece scold them, she came at once to their defence: 'Let the children look as nice as they can; I like to see the young have ideas of their own and your daughters seem to have taste.'[6]

Processions, balls, banquets and other such public appearances all gave the sisters a chance to deck themselves out in their finery, and revel in the admiration of Romanov cousins and Russian officers. A little harmless flirtation, as they saw it, was all part of the fun.

In Ducky's case, however, it went beyond flirtation – where her cousin Grand Duke Cyril Vladimirovich was concerned.*

Grand Duke Cyril was born at Tsarskoe-Selo on 30 September 1876, second son of Grand Duke Vladimir

---

*When the Grand Duchess of Hesse and Grand Duke Cyril first met is disputed. According to Hannah Pakula, *The last Romantic* (p. 99), they had already been in love for three years at the time of Ducky's wedding, in other words since 1891, and had doubtless known each other before that. However, Cyril's memoirs, *My life in Russia's service – then and now* (p. 112), state that their fourth meeting was in 1900, and refers to previous occasions in 1899, 1897, and at the coronation in 1896, which he therefore infers was the first.

(the third son of Tsar Alexander II) and Grand Duchess Marie Paulovna, by birth a princess of Mecklenburg-Schwerin. Cyril's elder brother Alexander had died in childhood; there were two younger brothers, Boris and Andrew, and a sister Helen, later wife of Prince Nicholas of Greece, one of whose children, Marina, later became Duchess of Kent. Cyril, a bachelor, was barely two months older than the cousin with whom he was shortly to become involved.

His parents had a reputation for being clever, artistic, wealthy and ambitious. They were both Anglophobes, their antipathy to Queen Victoria having been coloured by what they considered to be English ill-treatment of their sister Marie, but apart from this hatred of England they had little in common with the Tsar. Vladimir was jealous of his brother's inheritance; the Tsar had looked on Vladimir with contempt, and a degree of suspicion, on account of his dilettante interests. Grand Duchess Vladimir was intensely pro-German, and an ardent supporter of Bismarck and Emperor William II. Alexander III's attitude to the upstart German Empire had been strongly influenced by his virulently anti-German, Danish-born wife Dagmar, Empress Marie, who had never forgiven Bismarck and his fellow-countrymen for taking the duchies of Schleswig-Holstein from Denmark by conquest during the war of 1864.

While Missy, by her own admission, was 'gay and always amused', the apparently sombre, melancholy, rarely-smiling Ducky was better at concealing her feelings from the world around her. That the attraction between Cyril and herself was about to ripen into something deeper remained a closely-guarded secret.

'Of all the Royal beauties,' wrote Cyril, describing the coronation guests, 'the daughters of the Duke of Edinburgh were among the most radiant.'

That autumn, the young Tsar and Tsarina came to stay

at Wolfsgarten. It was an experience that neither guests nor hosts enjoyed at all. The earnest Nicky had no common ground with Ernie, and it was soon evident that they disliked each other's company; as for Germany, Nicky, who shared his mother's prejudices, found the country 'dark and boring'. Alicky, meanwhile, saw flaws in the marriage of which she had never approved in the first place, and differences in the outlook of both women were quick to surface. Ducky found Alicky rather stuffy, and criticized her for her narrow-minded devotion to *Kinder, Kirche, Kleider und Kuche.* When Alicky retorted that home life must always come first, Ducky answered that that was an old-fashioned Prussian idea.

Still the close relationship between Ducky and Missy endured. Both still sorely missed each other when apart; both had become mothers, yet they were married to men whom they did not really love. Missy was resilient enough and prepared to make the best of an unpromising marriage, but Ducky was unable or merely unwilling to come to terms with her unhappy situation. As ever, she sought comfort in diversions.

Yet Ernie still accompanied her to Roumania, when she paid her first visit to Missy there in the spring of 1897. Missy recalled afterwards that their joy at:

being together and sharing all things again, knew no bounds. We were probably looked upon as two frivolous young ladies, and were no doubt severely criticized by those wiser and steadier than we were. But for both of us it was a period of magnificent enjoyment which the disapproval of others could not mar. There is a superb daring about youth, which is admirable in its way; barriers and obstacles only heighten the desire to overcome, break through and win.[7]

Despite the problems in both marriages, the visit was a great success. In fact, the less than satisfactory husbands seemed to benefit from each other's presence. Ernie was a delightful companion, restless, full of life, ready to enjoy all the social delights of court life, such as Bucharest could produce, and 'could also be a clever inventor of varied amusements'. His vitality was infectious and he helped to stir the withdrawn, apathetic Crown Prince of Roumania a little. In awe of his uncle King Carol, to a degree which had sapped his character and undermined his self-confidence, Nando needed people around him such as the lively Grand Duke of Hesse, to give him some measure of self-assurance and encouragement to 'let himself go'.

Missy and Ducky adored dancing, and participated in court balls with relish. For them, the highlight of the season was a costume ball at the Cotroceni Palace. Unknowingly, both had chosen to appear as the same character, Princess Lointaine, a character from an Edmond Rostand play made famous by Sarah Bernhardt. As they had kept it a secret from each other, it came as a great surprise to all, especially as they were in similar costumes. The difference was that Ducky's was white with large pearly lilies worn over the ears, while Missy wore black and gold Indian tissue with red roses instead of lilies. However this could not detract from a most enjoyable evening, though the long clinging gowns were difficult to dance in and they had to change before the cotillion. This time, they arranged first what each was going to wear. Ducky reappeared as the moon, Missy as the sun.

These court balls at Bucharest, which were rare events under the regime of the stern, unbending King Carol, were grand official functions. Mothers brought their daughters; everybody dressed up, even the ministers, who all made an effort to cast aside their grave demeanour and enter into the spirit of the evening. But the more weighty personages did not stay very long; 'gradually the crowd thinned,' said Missy, 'and we danced till our feet ached.'

Ducky and Ernie extended their visit to Roumania by several weeks longer than planned. The sisters enjoyed their riding as much as ever, and spent part of nearly every day in the saddle. In the pre-motoring age, it was customary to ride on the Chaussee, the Bucharest high-life promenade of its time. There were many smart carriages and fine horses, and towards evening all the *elegantes* would drive up and down the avenue wearing their latest fashionable Paris toilettes, very showy with exceedingly ornate hats. It was the custom to trot down the length of this road at a very quick pace; most of the horses were Russian trotters, coal-black with long flowing tails. The way back was taken at walking speed, so as to let the horses regain their breath and to allow a mutual review of the ladies' smart dresses.

Ducky and Missy regularly took part in this unofficial parade, and would dress up in special tight-fitting riding habits, made from white drill with matching white boots, careful to ensure that their gowns, hats, cloaks and parasols should be in harmony. Their favourite hats, which they called their 'Empress Eugenie hats', were made of black felt, boat-shaped, with one long white and one long black plume.

They made a striking couple. Count Bernhard von Bulow, later German Chancellor, later recalled that 'a prettier picture could not be imagined than Grand Duchess Victoria, side by side with her blonde sister Maria [sic].'[8]

The men also drove out on the Chaussee, but not with their wives. When Ernie and Nando took to their carriage, they would politely salute the sisters, who 'answered with becoming grace'. In one respect the women were denied a privilege granted the men; in the princes' carriage, beside the coachman sat a green and silver-clad chasseur with long plumes flying from his bicorn hat, while Missy and Ducky had to content themselves with a mere footman.

The self-confessed 'frivolously-inclined giddy sisters' tormented Nando to allow them to drive out with the chasseur just for fun. A stickler for etiquette and male prerogatives, Nando retorted that only male members of the royal family were permitted this privilege. Undaunted, they persuaded a mischievous young officer to don the uniform of King Carol's chasseur one day. Ernie had been let into the secret, and everybody's rides on the Chaussee that day were timed to best effect. Nando had a special salute which was reserved for his sovereign, and the sovereign alone. When he recognized the man in King Carol's uniform driving past, he raised his hand to salute, and only then did he see to his disgust that the gesture was not honouring his august uncle, but instead his wayward young wife and sister-in-law. With difficulty, Ernie persuaded him that it had been a harmless little joke, and if he really wished to punish them, it would be far more effective to ignore their transgression completely. All the same, Nando gave them a severe scolding that evening, but Ducky and Missy felt that it had been well worth it, in order to see the horrified look on his face.

On other days, the sisters took pleasure in hunting out the more picturesque parts of Bucharest, older parts of the town, far away from fashionable society. They would haunt streets with odd little shops in which they could buy quaint objects in locally-produced leather, wood, pottery and metalcraft, returning with their carriages piled high with these strange acquisitions at which the servants scornfully turned up their noses.

In time they discovered for themselves a whole new world, far removed from anything they had seen or encountered in their sheltered childhood. There were quaint old houses with wood-shingled roofs, padded with great lumps of moss; half-forsaken old gardens; strangely solitary squares paved with round cobblestones; churches of unusual architecture and lonely-looking graveyards behind crumbling walls; and old stone crosses at odd corners of the roads. On the outskirts of Bucharest they found gipsy camps, at which they would dismount and penetrate fearlessly among the tents, climbing over piles of 'indescribable refuse', gazing about with interest. Almost at once they would be surrounded and pestered by hordes of children, holding out their hands and clamouring for money.

After the dancing season was over, Ernie returned to Germany – alone. For Ducky could not bear to tear herself away from her beloved sister, in this new country where she could behave more or less as she pleased, without being expected to conform to the code of behaviour expected of a *Landesmutter* at Darmstadt. It was far more enjoyable to go on long carefree picnics in the countryside, or to ride and explore the nearby woods and villages, than to go home again. Nando generally accompanied them, but like Ernie he did not enjoy riding. He invariably complained that the horses went much too fast for him, but his protests went unheeded.

Word filtered back to the Duchess of Coburg, who was always ready to admonish her daughters, criticizing them for appearing only too pleased to get away from their husbands:

> Flirt, amuse yourselves, but don't lose your heart,
> men are not worth it and if you could, *really* could
> see their lives, you would turn away in disgust, for
> you would find there nothing but dirt, even in the
> lives of those who seem to you good and noble.[9]

Yet it was not disapproval on the part of the elder generation that interrupted this lively interlude for

Ducky and Missy, but instead a breakdown in Nando's health. In May 1897 he took to his bed with what was diagnosed as typhoid fever, complicated by double pneumonia. After being at death's door for several days, he made a slow recovery, but he and Missy were unable to travel to England to take part in the festivities for Queen Victoria's Diamond Jubilee.

As many of the family as possible had been invited to London for the celebrations, Ducky and Ernie among them. Ducky had been looking forward to seeing her sister there yet again, doubtless so the two of them could enliven the solemnity of the august proceedings with their customary pranks. Probably to Ernie's great relief, this was denied her. It was therefore in a sombre frame of mind that she went to London.

Added to anxiety about Nando, and fears for her sister should she suddenly be left a widow, was deepening resentment of Grandmama's power and control over her family. She was tired of Ernie's incessant admiration of 'My own darling Grandma', and his cheerful, unquestioning submission to her wishes. Above all, the thought of divorce had entered her mind, and 'darling Grandma' was most unlikely to countenance divorce in her own family.

At the Buckingham Palace dinner held on 21 June 1897, the day before the Jubilee procession itself, guests were seated at tables of twelve each. Ducky and Ernie had been placed to sit at the Queen's table, Ducky herself being seated between the Crown Prince of Siam on her left, and Grand Duke Serge of Russia on her right. It was as if Grandma particularly wanted to keep a close eye on these two grandchildren in more ways than one.

Despite her advancing years, the Queen still took a special, and very well-informed, interest in the younger generation. She longed to hear of the impending birth of a male heir to the Grand Duchy of Hesse. To Princess Louis of Battenberg, she had written (October 1896):

> Your account of Ducky gave me great pleasure and
> I am sure she will become of more and more use
> to Ernie and she should be able to hold her own to
> be of use to him. I hope there will be another Baby
> – a Son, let us hope. Is there *nothing* coming?[10]

Despite her strictures, the Duchess of Coburg seemed to be more amused than shocked by her second daughter's waywardness. As she had never really approved of the marriage in the first place, she took some measure of malicious delight in seeing how much what she disdainfully called 'the English camp' were disturbed at its evident failure. Ducky was more Russian and less English in her inclinations than Missy, and for this the Anglophobe Duchess could forgive much. She too attended the Jubilee celebrations, but with great reluctance, and complained endlessly in letters to Missy (still bitterly disappointed that she could not be there) of the dizzy schedule of activities, the heat of London, the inferiority of English theatre, and above all about her husband's relations.

There were, however, certain members of the family to whom the Duchess did not object in the very least – her own. Among those staying at Clarence House were three representatives of the Romanov dynasty – Grand Duke and Duchess Serge (formerly Princess Elizabeth of Hesse, Ernie's sister), and Serge's nephew Grand Duke Cyril, paying his first visit to England.

Like his host the Duke of Coburg, Cyril was strongly attracted to the navy. Earlier that year he had joined the ship *Rossyra*, which had made a maiden voyage to England by way of Jutland, putting in at Devonport for a new coat of paint to make her spick and span for the Jubilee review at Spithead.

With pride, Affie led Cyril up to meet the Queen, with the words, 'May I present to you my young nephew, who is on a Russian battleship.'[11] Cyril greatly admired the British Navy; writing of a sojourn at Malta (as he would later note with hindsight, another great coincidence) a few months later, he remarked with envy on the smart evening kit of British naval and military men, and by the elegant dresses which their ladies wore at social functions. 'We had nothing of the kind in our navy, no mess jackets at all, and must have appeared a pretty poor lot to them.'[12]

It was a thoroughly discontented Grand Duchess of Hesse who returned to Darmstadt that summer.

CHAPTER 5

'A terrible and unexpectedly grave event'

*I*n a small town like Darmstadt, it was impossible to keep secrets. Rumours spread from the small court to military circles, and citizens of the grand duchy. The differences between their ruler and his wife were well known. It was said that he was visiting a lady in the town, and that he also showed a marked fondness for male kitchen hands and stable boys. As for her – well, she appeared to have a particular place in her heart for one of her Romanov cousins, Grand Duke Cyril.

With her remarkable knowledge of whatever went on among younger members of her family, Queen Victoria was equally aware that all was not well. At an audience with the Queen while on a weekend visit to Windsor early in 1898, Sir George Buchanan was visibly embarrassed at being unable to conceal from her how tense relations were between her grandchildren. After speaking about the Grand Duke and Duchess at some length, although he chose his words with great care, she remarked sadly, 'I got up that marriage. I will never try to marry anyone again.' She then proceeded to ply him with questions. When he answered that he had always tried to do his duty both by Her Majesty and by the Grand Duke and Duchess, and that he trusted she would understand how difficult it was for him to betray their confidence by repeating what they had told him, she said at once that she quite understood, and she was very grateful. Before

Sir George and Lady Buchanan left Windsor on that
occasion, they received a charming letter from the
Queen, enclosing two Jubilee medals as a mark of her
gratitude for their great kindness to her grandchildren.

Family matters provided Ducky with a heaven-sent
excuse to leave Darmstadt at regular intervals. Though
her parents' marriage had virtually fallen apart in all but
name, invitations were sent out far and wide for relatives
to join them at the Gotha Schloss to celebrate their silver
wedding in January 1899. They came to offer their
congratulations to the Duke and Duchess of Coburg at a
special ceremony in Schloss Friedenstein, followed by a
grand family dinner and gala theatre performance.

Yet the heir to the duchy was conspicuous by his
absence. Ducky's brother Alfred lay 'pale and emaciated'
in a room on the lower floor of the Schloss. The official
version of events, accepted unquestioningly by those who
knew no better, was that he was suffering from consumption.

This concealed the truth in a remarkably well-kept
royal secret. Young Alfred had led a riotous life ever since
being appointed to the 1st Regiment of Prussian Guards.
With a frequently absent father, and a mother who
mistakenly believed that the only way to get the best out
of her children was to scold instead of praise them, he
lacked all sense of encouragement, let alone any steadying
parental influence. Being placed at the mercy of a governor
who took every opportunity to ridicule him in front of
others, and a military aide whose pernicious influence led
him into the bad ways that he would have been introduced to anyway by his Prussian fellow-soldiers, but at a
less impressionable age, he never had a chance.

He might have been saved from a life of debauchery
and excess by a suitable marriage, but instead, it appears
– although the facts are still shrouded in mystery – that
he married an Irish commoner, Mabel Fitzgerald, at

Potsdam in 1898. Under the Royal Marriages Act of 1772 this match was invalid, and the Duchess of Coburg insisted that the marriage be annulled. Mabel was expecting their first child, and the father-to-be pleaded in vain against his mother's decision. He shot himself, although the wound did not prove immediately fatal. But his presence in the Schloss while his mother revelled in the limelight during the silver wedding celebrations was a dire embarrassment.

The Duke of Coburg, his health deteriorating after several years of heavy drinking and smoking, and the first signs of what would be diagnosed too late as cancer of the larynx, played a curiously negative part in the last days of his only son. It was his wife who brushed aside the objections of doctors, who told her firmly that he should not be moved from his sickbed or he would die within the week. Declaring that she knew what was best for her son, she sent him off to Meran in the Austrian Tyrol, with a tutor and medical attendant, to convalesce far away from home, in order that the embarrassing truth should not come out. Meanwhile, she arranged for him to spend a few weeks after that wintering in Egypt, in the company of Ducky and Ernie. In view of the deteriorating relations between them, this can have hardly been a comforting prospect for the invalid.

Such plans were in vain. On 6 February, a telegram reached the family to say that Alfred's sufferings were over. The truth had been concealed from his sisters, who were told (as was the press) that he had died of consumption. When Ducky and Missy learnt what had really happened, they were shattered. The Duke and Duchess were racked by guilt at having left their son to die so far away with none of the family beside him. The Duke held his wife responsible; already in poor health, his son's death left him a broken man. He was determined to lead what remained of his life as far away from her as possible, never to spend another night under the same roof if it could be avoided.

Ducky and her sisters attended the funeral on 10 February. Not since the news of Tsar Alexander II's assassination reached them in 1881 had they ever known their mother so demonstrative in her grief. At the sound of the funeral march, she fell to her knees, making the sign of the cross and sobbing violently.

Whether this family tragedy helped to bring Ducky and Ernie closer together can only be guessed at, but it is apparent that they made a determined attempt at reconciliation soon afterwards. They were among family guests at a dinner at Windsor held to celebrate Queen Victoria's eightieth birthday in May, and they followed her to Balmoral for a holiday at the end of the month.

The Queen went out of her way to pay special attention to her little Hessian great-granddaughter. An entry in her journal for 24 May 1899 noted that 'Beatrice came in early with a beautifully sweet nosegay, and then fetched darling little Elisabeth to wish me many happy returns of the day.' This girl of four eagerly appreciated the devotion shown her by the little old lady in a bathchair, huddled in her shawls, who could still provoke terror in her adult children and grandchildren. Meriel Buchanan recalled playing games one day in the palace nursery with Elizabeth, who was instantly distracted by the sound below of a pony carriage. Running out of the open window onto the balcony, she waved excitedly, calling, 'Granny Gran, I'm here' as the Queen drove past, looking up and acknowledging her greeting with a smile.[1]

On Deeside, Ducky immersed herself contentedly in her painting and drawing. To Marie Mallet, one of the Queen's ladies-in-waiting, this talent came as a great surprise. Where royalty was concerned, Marie could be extremely critical if not downright scathing, but for the Grand Duchess of Hesse, she had nothing but admiration. She thought her a particular genius in the field of decorative art, and maintained that she could make a very good living by designing wallpapers and chintzes. 'She draws unerringly, never rubbing out or correcting a single line, and her taste is excellent. It really is genius thrown away but it makes her very happy and she works as hard as if her livelihood depended upon it.'[2]

Ducky helped Marie and cousin Victoria ('Thora') of Schleswig-Holstein with preparations for a charity bazaar at Bagshot to be held in July, where every article sold was to be 'of Royal manufacture'. It was a reflection of the fondness Ducky genuinely had for Britain, despite impressions that she sometimes gave others to the contrary, that Marie could comment on the Grand Duchess and her 'loathing of Germans'. Though anything but British by birth, Marie noted, the Grand Duchess of Hesse 'adores England with passion and declares a cottage here is preferable to all the Schlosses in the Fatherland.'[3]

Ernie left separately for Darmstadt, and Ducky was due to follow him a few days later. On 10 June 1899 she telegraphed to the Queen from Buckingham Palace to say how she felt 'quite homesick for lovely Scotland',[4] and later that day a telegraph reached her from home that the Grand Duke had been taken ill. She left immediately, and shortly after her arrival at Darmstadt she was vaccinated, and not allowed to see her husband who had smallpox. Another telegram from Ducky to the Queen (14 June 1899) told her that:

> Ernie getting on admirably such an infinite relief,
> weather stormy, cold. Live quite alone with Baby
> and Wilhelmine and long to be able to talk to you
> like in the happy time at Balmoral, no question yet
> of being allowed to see Ernie.[5]

Not until a joint telegram (27 June), to say 'We are so happy to be together again', was Ernie restored to health.

The marriage of the Duke and Duchess of Coburg had already broken down, and though that of the Grand Duke and Duchess of Hesse gave every outward appearance of having mended, it now looked as if a similar fate was about to befall the Crown Prince and Princess of Roumania. Missy had been forced to employ a governess for her eldest son, an ugly, brusque-mannered British woman who delighted in stirring up trouble in the Cotroceni Palace. Between them, she and Queen Elizabeth exaggerated Missy's friendship with a handsome young male officer, Zizi Cantacuzino, into a major scandal which was only brought to an end when King Carol exiled Zizi and sent his heir's daughter away from Roumania on indefinite leave. She was carrying her third child at the time, and for once her plight touched the often hard heart of the Duchess of Coburg, who invited her back to Gotha. All the sisters were together again for Christmas 1899, and in the second week of January Missy gave birth to a daughter, also named Marie, but who would ever afterwards be known as Mignon.

By the spring, it seemed as if Princess Elizabeth would soon have a baby brother or sister. But Ducky had still not learned to play the passive part of an expectant mother, and she would not curb her riding activities.

After a brief sojourn in the Mediterranean, Sir George Buchanan wrote (15 May 1900) to Sir Arthur Bigge, the Queen's private secretary:

The Grand Duke and Grand Duchess appear to have derived much benefit from their stay at Capri and to have enjoyed it thoroughly. Their Royal Highnesses are both looking remarkably well and are very glad to be back at Wolfsgarten after their long absence. The Grand Duchess is naturally

obliged to lead a very quiet life at present, but the
Grand Duke has had a good deal to occupy him
since his return home.[6]

Ducky had already had one miscarriage, and despite
leading 'a very quiet life', the result was to be a prema-
ture stillborn son, much to her grief and no less to that of
her husband. Sadly but not without a note of optimism,
Queen Victoria referred in a letter (10 June 1900) to
Princess Louis about 'the disappointment at Darmstadt',
but hoping that 'as she is so much stronger we shall have
another event before too long which will repair this
blow!'[7]

Their cup of sorrow was not yet full. That same month,
their worst fears about the Duke of Coburg's health were
confirmed. He had cancer of the throat, and his condition
was inoperable. Marie Mallet remarked rather unkindly
that his life was not one to be accepted at any insurance
office.

The family were anxious to keep the news of his illness
a secret, largely out of consideration for Queen Victoria.
Now aged eighty-one, her health was beginning to give
cause for concern. As she herself remarked in her journal,
1900 was 'a horrible year, nothing but sadness and
horrors of one kind and another.'[8] There were the losses
of British soldiers, and international prestige, in the Boer
War; the narrow escape of the Prince and Princess of
Wales from an anarchist's bullet in Brussels; the assassination of King Humbert of Italy; and, perhaps most
distressing of all, the sufferings of the Empress Frederick,
whose suspected cancer of the spine prevented her from
visiting her homeland once again. Though Ducky had
been warned of the gravity of her father's condition, to
inform Queen Victoria that her second son was dying was
something they could not bring themselves to do.

By now in considerable pain, the Duke was taken back

to the Rosenau, his father's birthplace, where he too had spent his happiest hours on German soil. He had refused to see any members of his immediate family, but by now he was too ill to insist on such conditions. Ducky was summoned to his deathbed, as were Sandra, now Hereditary Princess of Hohenlohe-Langenburg, their mother, and Missy. The latter arrived too late, but the others were present as he breathed his last on the evening of 30 July 1900.

Six months later, on 15 January, the widowed Duchess of Saxe-Coburg arrived at Osborne with Baby Bee and her granddaughter Elizabeth. Though the Duchess's relations with her mother-in-law had rarely been cordial, the death of her husband and the Queen's declining health had made all the difference.

It was evident that Queen Victoria was unlikely to survive much longer. On 17 January, she suffered a mild stroke and lingered for another five days. On the evening of the 22nd, surrounded by most of her surviving children and several grandchildren, she passed away peacefully.

Princess Elizabeth was among those later brought in to see her great-grandmother's body laid out before it was placed in the coffin. Peering solemnly, she whispered, 'But I don't see the wings.'[9]

The Grand Duke and Duchess of Hesse were on a visit to St Petersburg when news of Queen Victoria's death reached them. It was announced in the Court Circular that they would leave Russia for England together on 26 January to attend the funeral, together with Grand Duke Michael, representing his brother the Tsar. Yet at the funeral at Windsor the following week, Ernie was present – but not his wife. Princess Elizabeth attended as well, sitting next to her cousin, Prince Edward of York, the future King Edward VIII. 'Sweet little David behaved so well during the service,' remarked his Aunt Maud, Princess Charles of Denmark, to the Duchess of York

(3 February 1901), 'and was supported by the little Hesse girl who took him under her protection and held him most of the time round his neck. They looked such a delightful little couple!'[10]

Despite all efforts made by the family at keeping the Grand Duke and Duchess of Hesse together, it was soon recognized that with their grandmother's death, the last barrier to their divorce had gone.* Their reconciliation had apparently ended with the birth of the stillborn son.

Invited to dine at Darmstadt a little later, Count von Bulow noticed how stiff and unfriendly the relationship seemed between husband and wife. 'Thank God I think we get on very well together,' Prince George wrote to his wife Princess May in 1901, 'and after what you told me the other day of the sad lives of Missy and Ducky.'[11]

In October, Ducky went to stay with her mother, and once she was there, she expressed her determination not to return to Darmstadt. She told Ernie that it was her intention to ask for a divorce.

Ernie readily agreed. To his eldest sister, Princess Louis of Battenberg, he admitted that the last few years had been a 'living hell':

Now that I am calmer I see the absolute impossibility of going on leading a life which was killing her (Ducky) & driving me nearly mad. For to keep up your spirits & a laughing face while

*Another granddaughter of Queen Victoria, Princess Marie Louise of Schleswig-Holstein, unhappily married to Prince Aribert of Anhalt, was in the process of having her marriage dissolved at the time. Yet she incurred sympathy rather than condemnation from her family, as it was evident that the unreasonable behaviour of her husband was solely responsible for the irreversible breakdown in relations between them.

ruin is staring you in the eyes & misery is tearing
your heart to pieces is a struggle which is fruitless.
I only tried for her sake. If I had not loved her so,
I would have given it up long ago.[12]

Princess Louis herself had foreseen the eventual out-
come for some time, and considered that she was less
surprised at the divorce than him. Both had tried hard to
make a success of their marriage, she saw, but in vain. By
character and temperament they were quite unsuited to
each other, and it was clear that they were gradually
drifting apart:

As I had known Ducky well from a child, since the
time that she lived with her parents at San
Antonio, she had often spoken freely to me on the
subject of her married life. She had confidence,
that I hope was not misplaced, in my fairness of
judgment and, in spite of my being devoted to my
brother, I can only say that I thought then, and
still think, that it was best for both that they
should part from each other.[13]

Not everybody was quite so understanding. To Tsar
Nicholas, such an eventuality had seemed impossible, as
he told his mother (27 October 1901):

I must inform you of a terrible and unexpectedly
grave event. Can you imagine – Erni and Ducky
are getting divorced, yes, actually divorced! We
heard of it three days before leaving Spala.
Victoria sent a long letter to Irene and Alix with
extracts from a letter of Aunt Marie's to her. In it
she explains to all her sisters that, as far as she
can see, the relations between Erni and Ducky had
been bad for some time past, that their

estrangement was growing from day to day and
that, in the end, divorce was the only possible way
out. Such is Aunt Marie's opinion and Ducky's,
too. Erni, after a long struggle, has come to the
same conclusion. It is all quite settled and nothing
left to do but for the ministers of Darmstadt and
Coburg to arrange the legal side. All of this
appeared to us so dreadfully sad and was so very
unexpected that at first we thought Victoria must
have gone out of her mind. But a few days later
Alix and Ella had the news confirmed by letter
from Aunt Marie, so that now there is no possible
doubt left. All that time, nothing from them direct
– not a word. At last, yesterday, a telegram from
Erni, saying that it is all definitely decided. I am
intensely grieved and sorry for poor Alix; she tries
to hide her sorrow. In a case like this even the loss
of a dear person is better than the general disgrace
of a divorce. How sad to think of the future of
them both, their poor little daughter – and all his
countrymen.

I enclose Aunt Marie's letter to Alix. She feels
responsible for having arranged their marriage
rather hurriedly; what a huge mistake it has
proved to be![14]

To the Grand Duchess of Mecklenburg-Strelitz, the
whole matter was almost beyond belief. 'What truth is
there in the Darmstadt divorce?' she wrote to her niece,
the Duchess of York (4 November). 'The Papers openly
speak of it; could they not agree? Ernie has been absent
some time, in Italy; what can it all mean?'[15]

On 21 December, the marriage was dissolved by ver-
dict of the Supreme Court of the Grand Duchy, on the
grounds of 'invincible mutual antipathy'. Provision was
made for the couple's daughter Elizabeth to live with her

mother for six months of the year, to spend the other six with her father, and to return to his court at Darmstadt when she reached adulthood.

As the Tsar's letter suggested, the divorce was considered a disgrace in royal circles, and almost without exception Ducky was held responsible. King Edward VII and the German Emperor were united in their condemnation. Although the Tsarina had never approved of the marriage, she was furious with the cousin whom she had always disliked, and maintained that her brother had been grievously wronged.

Though she had been prepared for censure, Ducky was angry at being treated as a virtual outcast by the family. Apart from her mother and sisters, and her ex-husband's understanding eldest sister, it seemed to her that everybody had taken Ernie's side. Many were the letters to Lady Buchanan, complaining of the uncharitable treatment they meted out to her. In self-defence, she claimed that she had sacrificed years of her youth because of her grandmother Queen Victoria's wishes, and surely she had a right to some happiness in life.

'My little Elizabeth was the sunshine of my life', Ernie recalled in his memoirs. His portrait of her describes a happy child, but with sad, anxious eyes, no doubt as she understood much of the unhappy atmosphere between her parents. She suffered as a result of the divorce, but stood by her father afterwards. Although he magnanimously told her that her Mamma loved her, she replied: 'Mamma *says* she loves me. You *do* love me.' Another time when she was with her father, she disappeared suddenly. Eventually he found her under a sofa, 'afraid of showing her grief'.[16]

How genuine this unbounded love was for her father, and apparent coldness for her mother, can only be guessed. Ernie felt immense bitterness towards Ducky after the divorce, and ordered the removal of as much material relating to her from the ducal archives as he could. It was therefore hardly surprising that his memoirs should seek to portray himself as an adoring father, and show his former wife in a bad light. Nonetheless, from all appearances he seems to have been the more conscientious parent of the two. To give Ducky her due, she was probably less ready for the responsibilities and burdens of parenthood at this age. Yet, as in so many other aspects of her life, she left no letters or diaries, let alone memoirs, to express any views to the contrary.

Elizabeth attended school at Darmstadt during the six months of each year spent with her father. To the people of the Duchy, the sight of this cheerful-looking little girl with long dark curly hair, driving out with her father, or running through the streets with a dog at her heels, was a familiar one. Sadly, not for long.

In the autumn of 1903, Ernie took his daughter on a visit to Poland, with the Tsar and Tsarina at Skierniewicz, staying in one of the imperial hunting lodges. The four Grand Duchesses, of whom the eldest, Olga, was Elizabeth's age, found her a ready companion on their picnics in the forest, walks and games in the palace corridors.

One morning, Elizabeth woke in agony, panting feverishly for breath. Ducky was summoned immediately by telegram from her mother's home at Coburg, announcing her daughter's illness. Another followed one and a half hours later, describing her condition as more grave, and shortly before midday, as she prepared to leave for Russia by train, a third one announced the girl's death. It was rumoured that she had eaten food from a poisoned dish intended for the Tsar, although an autopsy confirmed that she had died from typhoid.

Heartbroken, Ducky cancelled her journey. Equally prostrated, Ernie returned to Darmstadt with the coffin bearing the body of their child, to be buried at the

Rosenhohe. 'The melodramatic way in which she finally left Darmstadt which had respected her as its ruler for seven years did not reveal very good taste', Bulow noted. Although received with 'all honours' as she arrived for the funeral, this did not prevent her after the service from placing her Hessian Order on her daughter's coffin to show that she had made a final break with her old home.[17]

None the less, for Ducky it did mark a complete severance with the past. Already she had taken a decisive step into the future.

CHAPTER 6

'At last, the future lay radiant'

Even before her divorce, Ducky had found herself drawing closer to Grand Duke Cyril. For three years in succession, he was a welcome guest at Wolfsgarten. According to his memoirs, he was initially invited there in autumn 1899 by his brother Boris, who had received a personal invitation from Ducky. Evidently she had thought it discreet not to invite him directly herself. Cyril recalled that this visit was made particularly pleasant by 'amateur theatricals in the evenings at which all of us performed, rides and drives in the woods and pleasant pranks, and time passed only too quickly.'[1] Rather more surprisingly, perhaps, he noted that the visit must have been a success, for the Tsarina 'was particularly gay and charming, and gaiety was not part of her character'. This he put down, no doubt correctly, to the fact that Wolfsgarten contained memories of her youth, and she felt more at home in such familiar surroundings than at the imperial court.

Twelve months later, he was more specific about his hostess the Grand Duchess. Their friendship, he noted, was developing into strong mutual affection: 'The three weeks which I spent at Wolfsgarten in the autumn of 1900 were decisive for the whole of my life. Thereafter we were to meet as often as possible.'[2]

By 1902, as Cyril put it, the object of his affections was staying with her mother and sister Beatrice at Château

Fabron, Nice, 'in exile', when he next visited her. As Tsar
Nicholas II was head of the family, Cyril needed his
permission to marry a princess who was doubly ineligible.
Marriage between first cousins was contrary to the rules
of the Greek Orthodox Church; but this paled before the
stigma of marrying a divorcee.

Tsar Nicholas, a mild-mannered man, was fond of his
cousin. But in almost all things, especially where family
matters were concerned, he deferred to the wishes of his
wife, and this case was no exception. While Princess
Louis of Battenberg never wavered from her view that
divorce had been the only solution to the unhappy
impasse between her brother and his wife, the Empress
Alexandra felt that he had been grievously slighted.
Maybe she would have much rather seen them both put
up with a miserable marriage until death removed one of
them; but her devout religious principles would never
sanction divorce. That the former Grand Duchess of
Hesse and the Rhine should apparently cast aside her
(Alexandra's) brother in order to wed one of her husband's kinsmen and subjects was an unforgivable insult.
There was no doubt in her mind that the Tsar of all the
Russias should firmly refuse to countenance the very
notion.

Ducky therefore had to retreat in temporary disgrace.
Supportive though her mother and sisters were, they
could only advise her to bide her time. Missy in particular
was anxious that if Cyril defied the Tsar and was prepared to give up his country, career, wealth and family in
order to marry Ducky, eventually he would regret his
decision and take it out on her. Though he had a
reputation at home for being the bright dashing young
leader of the imperial 'smart set' at St Petersburg, 'the
idol of all women and the friend of most of the men',
Missy did not trust him. To her, he was 'the marble man'.
She found him particularly cold and selfish; 'he seems to

freeze you up, has such a disdaining way of treating things and people.'[3]

The only other member of the royal caste to offer any suggestion to Ducky was the impossibly theatrical Queen Elizabeth of Roumania. God, she declared, had 'moulded' her for sorrow. The former Grand Duchess, said the Queen, should 'go and learn how to nurse, form a sisterhood of her own, wander about the world in search of all the suffering, all the misery, all those that life has treated hardly. Lead a life of continual sacrifice, that her grand nature was destined for this.'[4]

There was little to be done to attempt to influence the Tsar in favour of Ducky and Cyril. Missy endeavoured to do so when she gave birth to a second son in August 1903, by naming him Nicholas and asking the Tsar to be his godfather, but though he eagerly accepted, the gesture failed to soften him.

While Ducky stayed with her mother at Coburg and in France, visiting Missy at intervals and helping her to paint and decorate her apartments at Cotroceni Palace, Cyril steeled himself for naval service on a long cruise in the Far East. Before setting sail, during a short spell of leave at Château Fabron, he and Ducky had had dinner one evening by themselves, with the full support of the Dowager Duchess of Coburg, being left alone as it was a farewell occasion:

She was in exile and I was going to the unknown,
to the uncertainty of a blank future. About one
thing both of us had no illusion whatever, that a
mountain of obstacles to our happiness would
arise, that every conceivable wheel of intrigue,
coterie and vetos would be put into motion against
us, and that we would be left to fight that sea of
troubles alone with thousands of miles between us.
By that time I would be at the other end of the

world and the woman I cared for would have to
defend herself as well as she could and I would be
unable to come to her aid.[5]

Feeling that this might be their last farewell, Cyril left
sadly to join his ship.

The following year, after his ship *Peresviet* docked at
Vladivostok, Cyril was handed a telegram from the Tsar,
informing him that he was to stay on in the Far East for
an indefinite period of time. He realized that pressure
was being brought to keep him and his beloved apart, and
reduce any chances of meeting her again. It was followed
by another despatch from his father, Grand Duke Vladimir, to the effect that he should submit for his own good.
In view of the fact that Vladimir was one of the uncles
whom Tsar Nicholas found intimidating at the best of
times, this was significant. Cyril was being requested to
subordinate his personal wishes to the cause of family
unity. Furious at the thought that plots were being
hatched behind his back, he felt that he was being
condemned to unofficial exile.

By Christmas 1902, he was in Singapore, where he
received a watch from Ducky as a present. The Russian
fleet spent three weeks based there, and mingled freely
with members of the British Pacific squadron in port.
Cyril made good friends with a British sloop commander,
who had served with Ducky's father and thus knew the
Edinburgh family quite well. Reminders of what, and
whom, he had been forced to leave behind were destined
to haunt him.

Next year they sailed back to the Mediterranean, and
Cyril received a message at Villefranche to the effect that
a steamer was to be put at his father's disposal. He saw
through this at once. As expected, Grand Duke Vladimir
came and tried, although 'by no means enthusiastically'
to persuade Cyril to give up all hope of marrying the

former Grand Duchess of Hesse. Seeing how obstinate Cyril remained, he gave in with good grace, whereupon Cyril went straight to Ventimiglia to meet her train. She had been staying in Switzerland and was on her way back to Nice.

Grand Duke Vladimir stayed in the area, and he had nothing but sympathy and good wishes for his son who was determined to marry in the face of such odds. He entertained the couple to suppers and luncheons, and appeared to be giving them his tacit support, no matter what the rest of the imperial family might think.

During the summer of 1903, after returning to Russia on naval leave, Cyril spent a few quiet weeks with his parents. Afterwards he went to the Rosenau, where he stayed with Ducky, Baby Bee, and their mother. From the account in his memoirs, they spent a blissful time together, savouring their freedom and planning for the future. They rode and drove a great deal, particularly in the forests near the castle. He took two cars with him, a small one and a large six-seater touring-vehicle resembling a clumsy kind of omnibus, equipped with a silver service for picnicking. Although it had six cylinders, it was far less efficient than the other, breaking down regularly.

Motoring in those pioneering days, he recalled,

> was accompanied by continuous trouble either
> from frequent breakdowns or from people and
> animals which one met on the way. Besides, cars in
> those days were the 'rich man's pleasure' and
> anyone having a car was naturally marked down as
> a capitalist, and therefore as an enemy of the
> people. I often met with some who manifested
> their outraged feelings in various ways of indignant
> behaviour as I passed by them. Apart from
> offending people politically there was another side

to the unpopularity of motor cars, one, indeed,
which had a more reasonable cause. They terrified
human beings and all manner of beasts. Chickens
were scattered in all directions, dogs run over,
horses shied, upsetting carts into ditches. There
were claims for damage done; road tolls had to be
paid. Frequently one was stopped by the police
and things had to be explained. In my
exasperation I had the number plate replaced by a
crown and fixed a special flag on the bonnet which
made things easier.[6]

Despite these mishaps, Ducky and Cyril enjoyed their
motoring trips immensely. They went through the length
and breadth of the Thuringian forest, and visited several
cities including Nuremberg and Gotha, discovering much
of old historic Germany for the first time. They also found
quiet spots and picnicked out in the open, 'far from the
busy world. Life was full and inviting. There was hope
and the joy of living which comes to one on such
occasions with the whole vigour and entirely carefree
spirit of youth. It was an appeasement after much anxiety
and sorrow.'[7]

While staying quietly with his parents at Tsarskoe-
Selo, Cyril had an interview with the Tsar, who refused to
give any indication as to the future prospects of a
marriage with Ducky, beyond a vague suggestion 'that
things would, possibly, straighten out'. As non-committal
as ever, 'he was very affable and showed much sympathy'.[8] The Tsar did however give Cyril permission to pay
a visit to Coburg. In accordance with imperial family law,
no member of the Romanov family, unless on active
service, was permitted to leave Russia without the sovereign's express permission.

At this stage, the Tsar's bland utterances about 'things
straightening themselves out' were probably a personal

hope that the infatuation between the young people
would soon blow over. As his letter of the previous year
had suggested, Ducky's divorce appalled and astonished
him. He probably thought Cyril would never dream of
asking him for permission to marry a divorced woman
whose previous husband was still living.

During 1904, two events stiffened the resolve of Ducky
and Cyril to become husband and wife. Russia's penetra-
tion of Manchuria and Korea led to an unforeseen attack
on the Russian fleet at Port Arthur in February, without
any declaration of war. Confident of easy victory over the
Japanese forces, Russia declared war, and Cyril reported
for active service. Before leaving for the Far East, 'and
plunging right into the midst of the witches' cauldron', he
obtained permission from the Tsar to pay a farewell visit
to Nice, where Ducky and her mother were staying. The
four days they enjoyed together resulted in an emotional
farewell, for each realized that it might be their last.

As first officer on board the flagship *Petropavlovsk*, Cyril
was fortunate to escape with his life when the vessel was
blown up by a Japanese mine while entering Port Arthur
on 13 April. Of the 711 officers and men on board, only 80
were saved. By the time Cyril boarded the Trans-Siberian
express home, he was in no fit state for further active
service. Badly burnt, the muscles of his back strained,
suffering from shell shock, and in a state of complete
nervous collapse, he was in his own words 'an absolute
wreck'.

On his return to St Petersburg, he was given an
enthusiastic reception as befitted a war hero, and a few
days later he had another interview with the Tsar. Tired,
overwrought, and visibly distressed at the progress of a
war which he and the ministers had been so confident of
winning, the Tsar made no enquiries about the loss of

Petropavlovsk, or about Admiral Makarov who had been killed on board. Instead he confined himself to pleasantries about Cyril's health and the weather.

Having secured permission to go abroad as soon as his condition permitted, Cyril left for Coburg and was met at the station by Ducky and Sandra, both dressed in white for the occasion. The reunion was indeed an unforgettable one. Feeling 'like one who was returning from the land of the dead to new life',[9] there was spring in Cyril's heart. Ducky's letters and telegrams had welcomed him back to Russia.

It was an exceptionally cheerful summer in Coburg for Ducky and Cyril. According to the latter:

> To those over whom the shadow of death has
> passed, life has a new meaning. It is like coming
> out of the darkness of a mine back to daylight.
> And I was now within visible reach of fulfilment of
> the dream of my life. Nothing could cheat me of it
> now. I had gone through much. Now, at last, the
> future lay radiant before me.[10]

Cyril's deliverance from an untimely death as one of the many Russian war casualties was one of his and Ducky's reasons for braving official wrath, and becoming husband and wife.

The other main reason was his displacement in the Russian succession. With the birth of four Grand Duchesses to the Tsar and Tsarina, Cyril was viewed as a probable successor to the imperial throne. This had been behind much of Vladimir's half-hearted attempts to dissuade his son. On 12 August 1904, however, a 300-gun salute at the Fortress of Peter and Paul, St Petersburg, announced to the Russian capital that a male heir had been born to His Imperial Majesty. Named after Tsar Alexis, this infant was the first male heir born to a reigning Russian Tsar since the seventeenth century. Amid the news of one débâcle after another on the Russo-Japanese war front, it seemed an omen of hope and of better times to come.

Cyril would have removed himself from the succession anyway by marrying a divorced cousin, but now that the Tsar had a son, his likelihood of succeeding to the throne was remote. He had intended to rejoin the Russian fleet again as soon as his recovery allowed. But in May 1905, as he was on his way eastwards, news arrived of the crushing Russian defeat at Tsushima. It was evident that hostilities with Japan would be concluded before long; Russia no longer had the resources nor heart to prolong the hopeless conflict. Cyril therefore sought the counsel of Father Yanishev, confessor of the imperial family. He assured the Grand Duke that, from the point of view of canon law, there was no obstacle to marriage with his divorced cousin.

Accordingly Ducky and Cyril spent the rest of that summer in Germany, mostly at Coburg, interrupted by Cyril's occasional visits to a sanatorium at Munich where he was still receiving regular treatment for his nerves. Germany was a considerably safer place for those of a nervous disposition in that ominous year of 1905. In February, a procession of petitioners, led to the Winter Palace in St Petersburg by Father Gapon, had been abruptly dispersed by gunfire from a panic-stricken police, resulting in about one thousand casualties on what went down in Russian history as 'Bloody Sunday'. A few weeks later, Cyril's uncle Grand Duke Serge, Governor-General of Moscow, was assassinated by an anarchist's bomb.

During the summer, Ducky and Cyril contented themselves with sightseeing throughout Germany, Cyril at the wheel of his car. From Munich they drove to Bayreuth, where they met Cosima Wagner, and later called upon

Ducky's sister Sandra and her family at Schloss Langenburg in Württemberg.

In Coburg, Cyril was almost regarded as a member of
the family. It had long been an open seret that he was
courting 'their princess', and intended to marry as soon
as the time was right. As they were unwilling to celebrate
their wedding while the shadow of war still hung over
Russia, they bided their time until peace was signed at
Portsmouth, New Hampshire, in August.

No Russian priest would dare to perform the marriage
rites, for fear of offending the Tsar and Tsarina. They
therefore chose the Dowager Duchess of Coburg's private
confessor, Father Smirnoff, to officiate.

On 8 October 1905 Father Smirnoff arrived at Count
Adlerberg's house at Tegernsee, near Munich. It was a
very simple occasion, with few guests. The only ones
present were the Dowager Duchess, her youngest
daughter Beatrice, Count Adlerberg, the Duchess's
gentleman-in-waiting Count Vinion, her two ladies-in-
waiting, and the Count's housekeeper. Cyril's Uncle
Alexis was in Munich at the time and Cyril wired to him,
asking him to come to Tegernsee as soon as possible, but
without telling him the reason. As Alexis had stood
beside him in his previous troubles, he particularly
wanted him to witness the wedding and held up the
ceremony, but when he failed to arrive, the ceremony
went ahead without him, in the Orthodox Chapel of the
house.

After the wedding feast had been in progress for about
half an hour, with a blizzard raging outside, Alexis
arrived. He had been chasing around Munich searching
vainly for a tarpaulin, and complained that the weather
had ruined one of the new suitcases piled up on the roof
of his car. When he discovered what had happened, at
first he was dumbfounded, then he congratulated the
newly-wed couple warmly, adding 'to the gaiety of this

occasion with his open, breezy personality and huge voice'.[11]

After a few days of honeymoon, Cyril left for St Petersburg with some trepidation to tell the rest of the family. The first to be informed were his parents, to whom the news came as little surprise. His father was particularly pleased. Cyril planned to tell the Tsar next day, but on the evening of his arrival Count Fredricks, a minister at court, came to see Vladimir while the family were playing bridge after supper. They guessed that this meant bad news, but nevertheless they were shocked when the Count presented the Tsar's ultimatum. Grand Duke Cyril, it announced, was to be deprived of his honours, struck off the imperial navy list, deprived of his income, and had forty-eight hours to leave Russia.

The shock was all the more acute, as during their previous meetings the Tsar had given no indication of any such measures. Indeed, he had expressed an apparently sincere hope that 'things could be straightened out'. It was not the first time that relatives and ministers, to their cost, had experienced the Tsar's fickleness.

Nobody was in any real doubt as to the true author of this punishment. To the Tsarina, remarriage, with a former partner living, was tantamount to violation of the seventh commandment. She had been angered by the publicity surrounding her brother's divorce, in which he had evidently been the wronged party, and when her former sister-in-law had the temerity to marry a close relation of her own husband, she declared angrily that she would never again receive a woman who had behaved so disgracefully; and her husband must be punished as well.

The rage of Grand Duchess Vladimir now knew no bounds. Like her husband, she had never cared for the young Tsar and Tsarina. This vindictive sentence turned indifference and veiled contempt into abiding hatred. To her uncle, Prince Henry VII of Reuss, she poured out her anger at this shabby treatment of her son. After describing the wedding, she told him that:

> The situation had become impossible and, since peace has come at last, Cyril was keeping his promise to wait till then. We have done all we could these last four years to hinder this marriage, but their love refused to be separated and so finally we considered it better both for Cyril's name and honour that the business should end with a wedding. We knew that the matter would not pass off very smoothly here, and were ready for some passing unpleasantness. But the blind vindictiveness and rage of the young Tsarina has, for sheer malice, exceeded everything the wildest imagination could conceive. She stormed and raged like a lunatic, dragging her weak husband along with her until he lent her his power and so made it possible for her to revenge herself on her ex-sister-in-law for marrying the man of her choice. The matter has been dealt with as though some terrible crime had been committed and judgment has been passed in this sense. Yet all these storms are directed against a Grand Duke, a war victim, a man who had made a name for himself at Port Arthur, who has chosen an equal for his wife, and who, instead of deserting him like the others, came here at once to take his punishment from the Tsar. It is too much that the son of the eldest uncle, of the man who, for the last twenty-five years has been the true and indefatigable head of the Army, who has saved the Tsar a hundred times, should be treated in this way at such a moment. One

unanimous cry of indignation has been raised by
all classes of the people. Vladimir has resigned as
a protest at the indignity of the treatment meted
out to his son. Even he, the truest of the true, says
he can no longer serve the Tsar with such anger
against him in his heart. The troops are in a state
of ferment at the loss of their beloved Chief, and I
know the Tsar is being warned on all sides how
dangerous it is to let his uncle go. That is why his
answer has been delayed six days. But I do not
think that Vladimir will consent to stay, even at
the Tsar's request, unless our son is rehabilitated.
What puts the last straw upon our patience is that
Cyril came here with the Tsar's sanction to
announce his marriage, and yet this very
appearance here has now been made his chief
offence. You, my dear uncle, will find this hard to
believe; but, alas, here everything is possible; and
when I add that this permission was given without
the knowledge of the Empress you will be able
perhaps to form a just idea of the position here.
This is how it was done; scarcely had Cyril arrived
when the House Minister came with an order that
he must leave Russia at once. The Tsarina wanted
him to go that very night but that would only have
been possible in a balloon! Then he was dismissed
the Fleet and the Army, he was to lose all uniforms
and rank, to lose his regiment which was conferred
on him at birth by his grandfather, to lose his
appanage, his name, his title. He was to go into
perpetual banishment. As far as his name was
concerned the Tsar had to retract a few days later,
since all the Ministers declared to him that this
could simply not be done. And why all this?
Because the Tsarina does not want her hated ex-
sister-in-law in the family. All the other reasons

given are mere formalities which could easily all
have been arranged, since even if we did not desire
this marriage there is nothing dishonourable about
it. We have suffered much and still suffer, and in
addition to it all I am worried about Vladimir's
health. The Tsar knows that strong emotions are a
danger to him. What does he care about that?
Think of us.[12]

Grand Duke Vladimir preferred more direct ways of
demonstrating his fury. He stormed into the Tsar's study
at Tsarskoe-Selo, demanding that his son should be
allowed to return home forthwith. Marrying a divorcee
without imperial permission was perhaps wrong, but to
be banished for a transgression which called for a verbal
caution at the very most, was quite out of order; no
member of the family had ever been punished so heavily
for such a trivial offence. The Tsar said nothing,
remaining calm and giving the impression that he was
trying not to listen. This provoked Vladimir into an even
worse rage, until he ended the audience by crashing his
fist down on the desk in front of his nephew, tearing the
decorations from his uniform and throwing them to the
floor, and bounding out of the room, slamming the great
gold-studded door behind him. A crack in the doorcasing
bore witness to the grand ducal fury.

It was all to no avail. The Tsar quietly accepted
Vladimir's resignation from his military offices, and Cyril
and Ducky were left in exile.

This treatment of Cyril caused great scandal in
St Petersburg. It had always been suspected that the Tsar
lacked a mind of his own; now, no further confirmation
was needed in the eyes of many that he was a weakling
under his hysterical wife's domination.

Battle lines were thus drawn between both branches of
the family. From that time onwards, observed Chancellor

von Bulow, 'the Grand Duchess Vladimir and her sons entertained towards the whole Court, the Tsarina, the Tsar, the sickly heir-apparent, those feelings which, from Philippe Egalité to Louis Philippe, the House of Orleans harboured towards the elder Bourbon line.'[13] The Grand Duke and Duchess Vladimir would never forgive or forget their sovereign's behaviour; this, coupled with the ambition that the Grand Duchess had always nursed for her sons, would colour her behaviour when occasion arose. And when Cyril and Ducky would be allowed to return to Russia, they would find themselves in the forefront of any question that might arise about the imperial succession.

CHAPTER 7

'Ta femme est
Grande Duchesse'

Cyril returned to Ducky, meeting her in Berlin and then going on together to Coburg. The Tsar had refused to confer on her the title of Grand Duchess. 'But the sudden vehemence of this storm did not mar our joy of being united at last,' Cyril recalled, 'and life lay inviting and happy before us.'[1]

Ducky seemed perfectly content for once, although Missy viewed the marriage with mixed feelings. Though she was glad that her sister was no longer single, she could not help wondering 'to what sort of happiness it will lead'.[2]

Despite the temporary loss of career and position, their three years of exile, their first three years of married life, were peaceful and serene enough. With Cyril's parents and Ducky's mother to support them financially, they divided their time between Château Fabron, Nice, where they spent each winter, a house in Paris, and Tegernsee, the Dowager Duchess of Coburg's home, which they used as a summer retreat. The first winter, however, found them at Cannes, from where they went to Strasbourg by car. Strasbourg was the home of Ducky's sister Sandra and her husband, Prince Hohenlohe-Langenburg, Viceroy of Alsace-Lorraine. Cyril occupied most of his leisure time playing golf which, said the Duchess of Coburg, he treated as seriously as others would sitting in parliament. Evenings would be spent visiting friends and playing poker.

In the summer of 1906 Ducky and Cyril emerged from discreet obscurity to attend their first public function, the Roumanian International Exhibition, held in Bucharest. During the exhibition they took their place with Missy and Nando, dining in festive pavilions hung with flags and lit with Chinese lanterns, overlooking a lake awash in floating lights.

Missy described their visit in a letter (12 July 1906) to Nancy Astor:

> My sister has left, the last part of the time she was
> not very well. She caught a mild form of cholerine
> and was very weakened by it and as she too is in
> the same state as you*I felt rather worried about
> her especially as she all the same stuck to the day
> she had fixed for starting. However they arrived
> safely at Coburg. I very much enjoyed their visit
> and felt very lost when she was gone. Towards the
> end all went very smoothly with the King and he
> even finally offered Kirill his highest decoration
> although Kirill is in disgrace with the Tsar. My
> sister and I knew how to appreciate this act of the
> King's because it must have cost him a great deal
> of thought and worry as above all he is a political
> man and always sacrifices any personal interest to
> his political views, that is what often makes life
> with him a very heavy business.[3]

Marriage to a man whom she loved, and for whom she had waited so long, had made Ducky a more placid, contented mother-to-be than the over-active young Grand Duchess who had tried to forget her problems by riding recklessly in the woods around Wolfsgarten.

* Expecting a child.

Shortly after Christmas and the new year of 1907, she was received into the Russian Orthodox Church. The move delighted her husband and her mother, who could not resist scolding Missy for not having done the same long ago on account of her children; 'one must take it seriously and your life is not like that,'[4] she chided her eldest daughter.

On 20 January 1907, at the Villa Edinburg, Coburg, Ducky gave birth to a daughter named Marie.

Soon after this, Cyril acquired a house in Paris, in the Avenue Henri Martin. They were here during the autumn of 1908 when they received a telegram announcing the death of Cyril's uncle, Alexis, and he (but not Ducky) was granted permission to return home for the funeral, obtained for him by his brother Boris. He had also been given permission to wear uniform for the ceremony. Afterwards, he spent a couple of days with his parents, then rejoined Ducky and baby 'Masha' at Cannes.

At length the Tsar had relented. 'I wonder whether it was wise to punish a man publicly to such an extent, especially when the family was against it,' he wrote to the Dowager Tsarina. 'After much thought which in the end gave me a headache . . . I telegraphed to Uncle Vladimir that I would return to Cyril the title which he had lost.'[5]

It was not merely a matter of the rest of his family being 'against it'. In fact, two of Tsar Nicholas's other close relatives – Grand Duke Nicholas (who would be Commander-in-Chief of the Russian army at the outbreak of the Great War), and his uncle Grand Duke Paul, had married divorcees themselves. His cousin Grand Duke Michael had married a commoner and settled in England, far from imperial jurisdiction. Cyril's brother, Andrew, was living with his mistress, Matilde Kchessinskya, who had borne him a son, Vladimir, in 1901. Ironically Matilde, prima ballerina of the imperial ballet, had been the mistress of Tsar Nicholas II himself before his betrothal. It was said that she threw herself at the Tsarevich's feet on the command of Tsar Alexander III, who had ordered her to make a man out of his timid, diffident son. Beside these misdemeanours and that of the Tsar's youngest brother Michael, who had gone abroad with a mistress who had divorced two husbands (both still living) and then given him a son, the behaviour of Ducky and Cyril had been virtually blameless. Had Nicholas II (and perhaps more importantly the Tsarina) maintained their sentence of banishment on Cyril, they would have found their court extremely thin on acceptable relations.

An even more powerful influence had come to bear on the subject. Though he had reacted angrily to the divorce in 1901, King Edward VII was prepared to draw a veil over the past. Throughout his mother's reign, he had seen too much family strife with sisters, brothers and cousins set against each other. He intervened on Ducky's behalf, probably by means of a friendly word when visiting the Tsar and Tsarina at Reval the previous summer, to suggest that the continued sentence of banishment on his cousins was unwise.

This was the least of the Tsarina's worries, for in addition her son Alexis, the long-awaited-for Tsarevich, had been diagnosed as haemophiliac at a very early age; and next in line to the throne was her disgraced brother-in-law Michael, temporarily in exile and sharing his house with a totally ineligible mistress. Now her cousin Cyril, third in line, whose courageous naval service had demonstrated that he possessed the leadership skills to make a worthy Tsar of the Russias, had had the temerity to marry the woman who had 'insulted' her brother.

Early in 1909, Grand Duke Vladimir's health deteriorated, and he died on 13 February. Shortly before his father's death, Cyril received a telegram from his mother to say that *'Ta femme est Grande Duchesse'*. He always treasured it among the few things he managed to salvage from Russia before leaving during the revolution. Ducky was thus created Her Imperial Highness Grand Duchess Victoria Feodorovna. Victoria was not a Russian name, and when a western princess came as a bride of a Grand Duke to Russia, her name was usually changed in keeping with family and church tradition. However, Tsar Nicholas II so revered the memory of his wife's grand-mother that he permitted her to retain the name with which she was born.

Amends had at last been made, though it was with a heavy heart that Cyril returned, too late to see his beloved father for the last time, or to attend the funeral.

On 26 April 1909 Ducky gave birth to a second daughter, Kira, in their house at Paris.

Later that year Cyril was appointed to the cruiser *Oleg* as her second-in-command. There followed the usual routine of fleet exercises and gunnery in the Baltic until the whole fleet returned to Kronstadt to be dismantled for its hibernation. *Oleg* was ordered to proceed to the Mediterranean, where a few ships were kept as part of the international squadron which guarded the Aegean, its base being Suda Bay, Crete.

Cyril went overland to Cannes, where Ducky and the two children were staying, and then to Brindisi, where he joined *Oleg*. After some uneventful service at Suda Bay, they went to the Piraeus and to Crete.

At last their rehabilitation was to be completed. In April 1910 Cyril was promoted to Captain, and when his ship docked at the Piraeus, he was given permission by the Tsar to take Ducky to Toulon on board. From Toulon she was to return to St Petersburg with the children, who had been in Cannes, while he continued homewards on ship. The following month, they both arrived on Russian soil – she at the capital, and he at Kronstadt. It was their first meeting in Russia, and the beginning of their married life in the country.

They were granted the use of the 'Cavalier's House' (Kavalersky Dom), at Tsarskoe-Selo, a splendid comfortable building with very spacious rooms. Soon after they settled into their new home, Ducky confided to Missy that she intended to learn to speak Russian, as she felt she was missing so much of what went on around her. It was unlikely, though, that she ever became proficient in the language.

That same month, Ducky's Uncle Bertie, King Edward VII, died at Buckingham Palace, aged sixty-eight, and was succeeded by his son as King George V. 'I too profoundly did not care for him to feel sad now, except at all old traditions', she wrote to Missy. She had never known him intimately, but felt somehow that it was the passing of an era:

> The whole world seems to lift up its voice and cry
> for the loss of a great King. But do you not feel as
> if the greatness only consisted in the startling
> comparison with the frivolous and notorious
> emphasis of his life as Prince of Wales. It is
> curious how little May and George are known in
> general. No Crown Prince and Princess have ever
> mounted a throne so entirely unknown to people
> abroad.[6]

In November 1910, Sir George Buchanan took up his appointment as British Ambassador to the court of St Petersburg. Ducky had kept up her correspondence with Lady Buchanan, and she was delighted that her old friends from Darmstadt days should be with her again. Her first audience with the family on their arrival in Russia filled her with unfeigned delight. She apologized laughingly for her 'bad behaviour' in the past, kissed Lady Buchanan warmly on both cheeks, talked of old days and memories, and particularly of her radiant happiness in her second marriage.

'Many were the pleasant evenings which we spent at their informal dinners and dances,' Sir George wrote later, recalling the hospitality of Grand Duchess Cyril and also that of the Tsar's sister, Grand Duchess Xenia. 'One of the most attractive traits in the Russian character was . . . its extreme simplicity; and all the members of the Imperial family were as simple and natural as could be. They never stood on their dignity and disliked being treated with too much ceremony. When they came to the Embassy it was always by preference to some informal entertainment, and what they liked the best of all was a *diner dansant* at round tables, where they could talk unreservedly to their friends.'[7]

During the reign of Tsar Nicholas II, there were several rival leaders of society. The Tsarina was totally unsuited by temperament and health to lead any sort of grand gathering. She could not and would not conceal her contempt for St Petersburg society, and what she regarded as its false glitter, indolence, love of pleasure, and scandalous loose living. 'Alix I haven't seen as she is again laid up,' Ducky wrote rather waspishly to Missy on Christmas Day 1910, 'or at least does not receive visits so once more there is no chance of court festivities this winter.'[8] The Tsar felt that it was his duty as sovereign to move into the Winter Palace for a few weeks each year and take part in 'the season'. Each January there was a ball to which members of the diplomatic service were invited; after that, lunches and dinners plus occasional receptions to which deserving subjects were bidden. Anybody to whose name was attached the merest whiff of scandal or grounds for censure was struck off the guest list, and this left very few.

Sir George Buchanan appreciated how much the Tsar would have loved to join in:

> I remember how, at the diplomatic reception on
> New Year's Day, 1912, after speaking to me about
> some political question, he said: 'My sisters tell me
> that they are going to your house tonight. Are you
> giving a ball?' On my replying that it was not a
> regular ball, but that we were giving a dinner of
> about a hundred and fifty persons at round tables
> and were going to dance afterwards, His Majesty
> exclaimed: 'What fun that will be.' I longed to ask
> him to come too, but knew that it would be
> useless, as neither he nor the Empress ever went
> into society.[9]

It was therefore to courts held by the Tsarina's less priggish rivals that others flocked. The Dowager Tsarina, still only in her late forties when her husband died, gave amusing parties at the Anitchkov Palace, renowned for the best French food and wine to be tasted in Russia. After her husband's death, Ducky's 'Aunt Miechen', her mother-in-law, Grand Duchess Vladimir, threw herself into a round of dinner parties and *soirées* in her palace at Ropsha, near Peterhof, on the River Neva. Her balls all but eclipsed the splendour of the Winter Palace, and her parties were almost oriental in character. In her patronage of the arts, she looked down on Gatchina as something of a provincial manor. Russian society loved her, and found her everything the Tsarina was not. She was well-dressed, well-read, intelligent, devoted to gossip and intrigue, and as ambitious as ever for her three sons so close to the throne.

Into this lively world, the Grand Duchess Cyril came not so much as a rival, more as a respected and valued participant. She got on very well with her mother-in-law,

whom she resembled so much in character and love of
fine clothes. According to Meriel Buchanan:

No party was considered complete without her, the
lovely – and very often unusual – clothes she wore,
were examined minutely, and sometimes copied,
the colour and decorations of her rooms were
discussed, admired, and envied, invitations to the
entertainments she gave were angled for
assiduously by everybody in society.[10]

Although Grand Duchess Vladimir and the Dowager
Tsarina never really liked or trusted each other, Ducky
was also fond of 'Minny', whom she always found 'kind,
delightful and attractive'. The balls and receptions Ducky
and Cyril gave were eagerly looked forward to by all – or
nearly all. Needless to say, they were never attended by
the Tsar and Tsarina. Yet the endless round of entertaining could sometimes become too much of a good
thing, as she told Missy (12 June 1910): 'They keep such
late hours here and as I stuck to getting up only because
of the children I find it often very fatiguing; night after
night to get to bed between one and two in the morning
never did suit us, did it?'[11]

Occasionally Ducky's efforts to help led to trouble. At
one stage she considered the idea of a match between
Meriel Buchanan and one of the Grand Dukes, 'Sandro',
Alexander, Duke of Leuchtenberg, whose grandmother
Marie was a daughter of Tsar Nicholas I. The two of
them partnered each other at a ball, dancing the cotillion, and he followed this up with a visit to her at the
embassy. Ducky made an effort to arrange things, but
his father refused to think of him marrying Meriel,
insisting that he must marry the daughter of an heiress
and not the daughter of an ambassador who had no
private income of his own. Lady Buchanan was much

relieved, and thought that the young Duke had behaved 'like a cad'.

Seeing the look of disappointment on Meriel's face after announcing the failure of her plans, Ducky sent her into the next room to entertain her daughters, who were on the floor building a toy castle. The collapse of this castle, with its rattle of bricks, sounded to Meriel's ears like 'the death-knell to all my dreams'.[12]

However, Ducky did at least one positive thing for Meriel which the latter never forgot. She gave her a Siamese cat called Fatima, as well as some long-sounding Oriental name, but inevitably abbreviated to Fatty. The cat was very good-natured, never scratching, spitting or growling at anybody. Although she had been intended for Lady Buchanan, she made up her mind that she belonged exclusively to Meriel instead. She would chatter to her endlessly, rubbing herself against her legs, until forcibly removed upstairs by one of the maids.

Ducky was also briefly involved in an abortive scheme to marry her eldest niece Elisabetha to the Duke of Montpensier. 'Yesterday I was officially asked to receive this gentleman whose letter I am sending you in the name of the Duke of Montpensier,' she wrote to Missy (10 May 1913). 'They very, very dearly desire this marriage with Elisabetha. You know that I myself could see no charm in this fiance . . . He is full of French show-off which of course to our natures is abhorrent.'[13]

While Ducky savoured a hostess's life, Cyril did the rounds of 'Court functions and social activities to attend, but they were, if I may use the expression, of a mild kind and nothing to compare with the brilliant occasions of Uncle Sasha's reign.'[14] Between 1910 and 1912 he served in the naval academy (the Russian equivalent of Greenwich), where officers received advanced instruction in technical subjects, or else prepared for admiralty work.

At the same time Cyril took a keen interest in an

automobile club, organized by car-owning members of the nobility of the Russian Baltic provinces. The club ran annual motor rallies, named the 'Victoria Fahrt' in honour of their patron's wife, and at these Ducky and Cyril were semi-officially received by members and hospitably entertained by owners of the castles which lay on the rally route. One castle they visited was Cremon, standing among pleasant surroundings overlooking the valley of the River Aa. Then they went to Riga, the capital of Latvia, before continuing their journey by car to Germany and Coburg.

Yet Cyril's active life in the navy was almost over. In the autumn of 1912 he was ordered with *Oleg* to the Mediterranean, but his nerves, or what he called 'the "evil" which pursued me in the shape of that ghastly and haunting awe of the sea came upon me again.' He had to leave the ship, and returned to Reval, where Ducky joined him and they spent two very happy weeks at the country place of the Orlov-Davidovs. On two subsequent occasions, he attempted to put to sea again, but the 'holy terror' of it prevented him from doing so. It was no use fighting fate, and he had to consider his career afloat at an end.

Ducky had always kept up her painting as a hobby. In the summer of 1913, the season of the Romanov tercentenary celebrations, she stayed with her mother-in-law at Tsarskoe-Selo, and painted a portrait of Meriel Buchanan, kneeling by a stone sarcophagus covered with white roses, black draperies around her, her face hidden in her arms.

While Meriel posed as a model, Ducky chatted to her and to Lady Buchanan, much of her conversation centring around memories of her former unhappiness, occasional outbursts against the 'stuffiness' of her English relations, in particular the Queen who had refused to hear of her divorce:

When I was young, Missy and I adored
Grandmama Queen. We used to think it a great
honour to be invited to go and see her. We loved
her bullfinch and all the photographs in her room,
but we thought her spaniel was too fat. And, oh,
how solemn her Court was. How tired I got of the
talk of 'Grandpapa in Heaven', and of the constant
mourning. And how I later resented the lectures
she was giving me.[15]

Friends and relations who knew Grand Duchess Cyril
well in later life recalled that she was, and claimed always
to have been, passionately pro-English. Yet at times, in
her resentment of the English court, she had certainly
proved herself a true daughter to her mother.

The last winter season at St Petersburg, 1913, was
always remembered as a particularly colourful one, as if
the participants and onlookers had some premonition of
what was in store for them. The greatest social event on
the court calendar was a fancy dress ball given by
Countess Kleinmichel, with several set quadrilles in
costumes of different periods, the most spectacular being
a Persian quadrille led by Ducky and her brother-in-law
Boris. Only young married women were officially permitted to take part, but Ducky insisted that Meriel should be
invited as a particular mark of personal favour.

During the following summer, Ducky had the joy of
welcoming Missy and Nando as her guests on Russian
soil. The Crown Prince and Princess of Roumania were
paying a semi-official visit to Russia, but not without
dynastic purpose; for it was hoped that Prince Carol and
the Tsar's eldest daughter, Grand Duchess Olga, might
become betrothed. In the event it came to nothing, for the
young people seemed indifferent to each other and the

young Grand Duchess was reluctant to make a marriage which would take her away from Russian soil.

Like so many other visitors before her, Missy was struck by the isolation of the court life that Tsar Nicholas II and his wife had created for themselves as the years advanced. Although the outward pomp and show of power of previous days still beckoned, at the front door of Tsarskoe-Selo this all ended, giving way to a threshold of uniform, exclusive and rather dull family life. Presided over by a shy, gentle, hushed Tsar and a prematurely aged, invalid Tsarina, whose chronic heart condition kept her in bed most mornings and confined her to a wheelchair for much of the time she was up, it could hardly be otherwise. Nicky, thought Missy, seemed to live in a sort of imperial mist, while Alix's forced smile of greeting and an instant impression of making even close relations seem as though they were outsiders, made even her contemporaries in age feel like children.

Ducky was not alone in telling her sister that the court at Tsarskoe-Selo was looked upon as a sick man refusing every doctor and every help. The Tsar and Tsarina had almost entirely shut themselves off from society, and even from their own kith and kin. The Tsarina was held responsible for this state of affairs, and the mysterious, dreaded Rasputin was widely mentioned as the *eminence grise* behind her behaviour.

Nonetheless, the Roumanian royal family's visit had apparently left its hosts in relatively good spirits, as a letter from Ducky to Missy (29 June 1914) suggested:

The Majesties and daughters & suites all came
back really thoroughly enchanted with their visit to
you – Alix also admitted how nice and hearty it all
was. I am so glad for you all . . . We are all getting
on nicely here. The weather has been monstrously
stupendously hot, up to 47 degrees in town and it

has been weeks without a drop of rain even. I've
had a busy time through all this heat with official
visits, the most amazing being that of the English
fleet commanded by Beatty. We had many a good
talk of olden days and he asked much after you.
He has rather a pretty wife who came on her own
yacht with their little boys. Beatty is quite
unchanged. We have a tiny little motor yacht of
our own on which we made a trip of several days
out in the Finnish waters amongst lovely islands,
unhappily it can only contain us two so we are
sending the children to the Finnish sea with the
last remnants of whooping cough. There we bathe
daily & enjoy it. It is in fact the only bearable time
of the day.

Our manoeuvres are late this year, last most of
Russian August so that we will not get abroad till
European September but I do hope we'll meet
then. Aunt Miechen has her Dutch brother staying
with her, a fat fair haired creature, quite gemutlich
but very German, something like 'der Furst' but we
don't allow anyone to develop their pomposity,
they are squashed in time. The life in Tsarskoie as
you know 'est tout ce que je n'aime pas' but the
place is lovely and sympathetic. I can't write more,
I am too hot, dripping and sticking at all angles.
I've never known anything like it.[16]

Although careful not to set herself up as the leader of a
rival court, Ducky was still regarded as a born hostess.
Her house, said Missy, was arranged beautifully and
filled with innumerable treasures, including a superb
collection of jade. She 'had perfect taste and ... (a
passion) for arranging her rooms in a rather unusual and
uncommon way'. True to form, she was still not
completely satisfied with her lot. She complained of the

want of light and endless St Petersburg winters, with their cruelly short days. Nevertheless she seemed more contented than before, and proud of her settled family life. To their Aunt Missy, or 'Maddy', as she was by now regularly addressed in correspondence, the girls Marie and Kira 'were two splendid children, well-grown, solid, with lovely hair and perfect skin and as superlatively groomed as English ponies.'[17]

Of the three great imperial hostesses of Romanov Russia in her sunset era – the two widows, Dowager Empress Marie and Grand Duchess Vladimir, and the latter's daughter-in-law, Grand Duchess Cyril – it must have crossed many minds that the last-named would have filled the imperial throne far better than its actual occupants. Whether Tsar Cyril and Empress Victoria Feodorovna would have averted or escaped the tragic fate that befell Russia and her first family at Ekaterinburg five years hence is of course a hypothetical question, though Ducky's obstinacy was tempered with more liberalism and commonsense than that of Alix. Yet they must have foreseen that the empire which had celebrated its tercentenary less than twelve months before was tottering, if not doomed; and, partly by good fortune, partly by an intelligent instinct for self-preservation, they were among the few who were not dragged down the precipice that swept so many of the family in its train.

CHAPTER *8*

'Nothing is left, nothing!'

Cyril's horror of the sea did not prevent him from enjoying a new luxury – a specially-commissioned motor yacht built in Southampton. In July 1914 it was despatched to him, with an English engineer and a crew of Russian naval guards on board. Cyril and Ducky used it for a little cruising, then going to take part in the annual motor rally in the Baltic provinces. They drove from castle to castle and finished up at Riga, where a gala banquet was given for them in the city's fashionable Strandt restaurant.

They were to go to Coburg the following day, and had made all necessary preparations for going to Germany, when during the banquet the Governor-General, M. Zvegintzov, arrived to read out a telegram announcing that Germany had declared war on Russia. This, Cyril remarked, 'produced the effect of a bomb on the gay gathering'.[1]

Immediately they left Riga for Tsarskoe-Selo in Count Serge Shuvalov's car. There was commotion and chaos on the roads, which were teeming with people, cattle and horses. Reservists were moving to the various rallying points, and mobilization was in full swing. As it was impossible to make proper progress by road, which was blocked with traffic, they took a train at the first available opportunity. The railways were in similar chaos, and they deemed themselves fortunate to complete the journey in a third-class railway carriage.

Although Russia and Britain were allies, the former country held the latter responsible for the outbreak of war in certain quarters at least. To the end of her days, Grand Duchess Olga maintained stoutly that if only King George V's government had made it clear from the outset that England would join Russia and France if Germany made trouble, Emperor William would never have dared to make a single move against them. The German ambassador at St Petersburg told the Russian imperial family that he was convinced Britain would remain neutral at all costs.[2]

During the first few days of the war, all private motor cars in Russia were requisitioned for ambulance purposes. Most Russian organizations, such as the Red Cross, schools and hospitals, were financed by members of the imperial family. Ducky threw herself wholeheartedly into nursing, and her motorized ambulance unit was one of the most efficiently-run services in Russia. For part of the time she was based at the front near Warsaw; 'unlike many others who were playing at Red Cross nurses,' wrote Cyril, 'she had chosen hard and practical work, and on several occasions had carried out her duties under the enemy's fire.'[3]

Not only her husband had praise for her efforts. At the Supreme Commander's headquarters, General Kondzerovsky saw her Red Cross train arriving at the front; he professed himself 'quite impressed by her energetic looks'. She regularly visited the front, often returning looking worn and harassed, her eyes heavy with lack of sleep and overpowering weariness. Acutely aware of the lack of organization in the Russian conduct of the war, she could see for herself the shortage of supplies, Red Cross material, and ammunition.*

*A few simple statistics will suffice to illustrate the plight of the Russian army. When General Mackensen launched a German offensive against the Russian Third Army in the summer of 1915, he brought up more than 200 heavy guns to open his campaign. The Russian army was stretched along some 130 miles of front, with

Ducky was no exception to the royal and imperial relatives who found not only cousins, but also sisters, on opposing sides during the conflict. As Hereditary Princess of Hohenlohe-Langenburg, Sandra and her husband were under the German flag. For two years, Roumania was neutral, and Ducky was eager for her and Nando to declare themselves on the side of the Entente powers. 'Ducky is furious that we have not joined them,' Missy wrote to Sandra in March 1915, 'and sends me insulting messages through the people who come here as only Ducky can produce in which she considers her frightful wrath against "those cowards!"'[4] Despite her Russian birth, the Dowager Duchess of Coburg had become passionately pro-German, and stoutly championed the cause of Germany.

Ducky fully shared in the ever-growing resentment of the Tsarina's influence, and anger at her appointment of Rasputin's protégés to commanding positions of government. In 1915, when Grand Duke Nicholas was relieved of his post as Commander-in-Chief of the Russian forces and replaced by the Tsar himself, and when Rasputin's cronies were appointed to government posts solely on the Tsarina's recommendation, she became more and more angry with her cousin, and resentment hardened into open hostility. All the same, she considered it her patriotic duty to go and see the Tsarina in order to try and reason with her. When told that she was meddling in matters which were not her concern, she

---

precisely four guns (two 4.2 inch guns, two 6-inch howitzers) between them. When the British military observer, General Sir Alfred Knox, arrived in Russia later that year, he observed 1,800 raw infantry replacements arriving at the front during one attack. None of them had his own rifle. They had been sent to reserve trenches to wait, in Knox's words, 'until casualties in the firing line should make rifles available'.

returned seething with exasperation, saying that she had been treated like an ignorant schoolgirl.[5]

The Tsarina's dislike of Ducky was intensified by Ducky's friendship with the Buchanan family. Sir George was not forgiven for his plain speaking to the Tsar, telling him how unwise it was of him to assume supreme command of the armed forces. She was convinced that the Grand Duke and Duchess Cyril, her widowed sister Ella, and the Buchanans, were all in league with each other, plotting to remove 'Our Friend' Rasputin, and suspected that Ducky was stirring up ill-feeling among their relatives abroad in her letters. Although it would have been unlikely for Ducky not to refer in scathing terms to Rasputin, she was circumspect enough, unlike her hot-tempered mother-in-law, not to make open remarks to the effect that the Tsarina should be 'eliminated or shut up'.[6]

Something drastic had to be done about Rasputin, and at length something was. In December 1916, he was lured to the house of Prince Felix Youssoupov and murdered, in a macabre conspiracy hatched by the Prince, and Grand Duke Dmitri, in an attempt to eliminate the Tsarina as a primary force in the imperial government. Dmitri and the Prince's valet completed the deed by dumping the still alive and semi-conscious peasant in the icy waters of the river Neva, in order to accomplish by drowning what cyanide-laced cakes and a volley of revolver bullets had failed to do.

Although Dmitri had always been one of the Tsar's favourite cousins, he was banished to the Persian border for service with the Russian troops. Dmitri was very highly-strung and suffered a nervous breakdown of sorts soon after leaving St Petersburg, and the family rallied round to help him. At Grand Duchess Vladimir's suggestion, they decided to send the Tsar a petition. After a meeting in her palace one night in January, sixteen members, including Ducky and Cyril, jointly drafted and signed a letter appealing against Dmitri's sentence, and begging that clemency be shown him in view of his tubercular condition. It was handed to the Tsar that night, and later returned with a terse note in his hand-writing to the effect that 'Nobody has the right to commit murder', and expressing astonishment that they should address themselves to him.

From his home in Kiev Grand Duke Alexander, cousin and brother-in-law of the Tsar, went to Tsarskoe-Selo to beg the Tsarina to withdraw from politics, and to ask the Tsar to grant a government acceptable to the Duma. To this, the Tsarina replied coldly that it was impossible for an autocrat to share his powers with a parliament. Alexander told her that His Majesty had ceased to be an autocrat in October 1905, when he granted Russia a new constitution. The interview ended with Alexander shout-ing at her that she had no right to drag the whole family with her down the precipice, and with the Tsar quietly leading him from the room.

The sympathies of King Carol of Roumania, a Hohen-zollern by birth, had been with Germany – unlike those of his government. However, he died in October 1914, a few weeks after the declaration of war. After clinging uncertainly to neutrality for two years, Roumania declared for the Entente in 1916. King Ferdinand's pro-German inclinations soon melted before the deter-mination of his government and even more so that of his wife, Ducky's elder sister Missy, once a passionately pro-English Crown Princess and now an even more passionately pro-English Queen.

Shortly before Christmas 1916, Ducky had arrived in Roumania to take medical supplies and provisions, as well as to make a visit to the sister with whom she had lost touch for a while. Feeling threatened on all sides by enemy nations surrounding Roumania, and with pessimism from all those around her, the Queen was badly in need of moral support, and Ducky's 'quiet, staunch, somewhat masculine personality'[7] was just what she needed. In distributing supplies, she proved Spartan and untiring. She and Missy looked for railway carriages which could be turned into hospital trains for the Russians, and at a hospital convent they both had a stormy interview with a cantankerous Mother Superior, exasperated as everybody was appparently trying to take her house from her. She was especially rude about the Russians, which made Ducky angrier still.

The Roumanian ministers and premier-foreign minister Bratianu asked Ducky to intercede with the Tsar, on whom the Roumanians felt their survival as a nation depended. The Russian troops should be begged to hold their ground, and to respect the Roumanian soldiers' rights. Inequalities between the two nations' forces had been highlighted by cases of Russians ransacking Roumanian warehouses and making off with all the best bread and meat.

After Ducky left, there was talk in Roumanian government circles of sending Queen Marie to appeal directly to the Tsar, until rumours reached the court at Bucharest of trouble at St Petersburg. With the elimination of Rasputin, and wild stories about the fate of the Tsarina, the time was evidently not right.

In January 1917, Ducky returned to Roumania. Her first visit had made a favourable impression on all with whom she had come into contact. Although Missy's glowing report that everybody was pleased that she had come back, as 'she is much liked, as all recognize her undeniable personality, her strength of character, and superior intelligence'[8] was bound to be biased in her favour, there was no doubt that Roumania respected the Grand Duchess Cyril. After wild rumours about the Tsarina, it was a relief for the government to find that at least one of their Romanov allies had her fair share of commonsense and leadership qualities. She brought further generous quantities of foodstuffs – sweets, tea, home-made cherry brandy, and smoked fish. There were useful articles of clothing like Russian water-tight boots, and fur-lined leather jackets. And there were inevitably more medical supplies, so badly needed by the hospitals for the wounded soldiers. Ducky needed all the warm clothing she could muster herself, for Roumania was bitter that winter, and on her drives with Missy in an open car to watch wood being cut around Jassy, she was a martyr to poor circulation.

To Missy she talked endlessly about the dangerous situation in Russia, and told her sister that the Tsarina was so hated that there was a strong possibility of her – and perhaps the Tsar as well – being suppressed in one way or another.

During those last days of imperial Russia, before insurrection and anarchy broke out in the stricken empire, there were rumours of a palace revolution being hatched by Ducky's in-laws. The late Grand Duke Vladimir, no admirer of England or of Queen Victoria's family, had been displeased when his nephew, Tsar Nicholas, had married one of the Queen's most English grand-daughters, though he attended the wedding. His widow, who fully shared his prejudices, was third lady of the Russian Empire, ranking only behind the Tsarina and the Dowager Tsarina.

Late in the previous year, she had allegedly attempted to bring a marriage alliance between her son Boris and his cousin Olga, eldest daughter of the Tsar and Tsarina. Boris had inherited his father's detestation of the English, and disgraced himself one day by getting drunk at the regimental mess in the presence of several officers from the British military mission, and making several wild accusations, one of them being that the British army was sitting in trenches on the western front while its French allies were being massacred. He was taken to task by General Sir Alfred Knox, the British commander, and later by the Tsar, and although he apologized under pressure, nobody was left in any doubt of his true feelings.

It was unlikely that Boris, a notorious womanizer, was in love with Olga. Though little is known of the projected match, the cynical Grand Duchess Vladimir probably saw it as a means of strengthening the claim of her sons to the throne instead of the sickly Tsarevich – particularly if the Tsar should abdicate. Similar dynastic manipulation in 1848 on the part of Archduchess Sophie of Austria, a similarly strong-willed woman who harboured the greatest ambition of all for her sons, had ensured after the abdication of her mentally defective brother-in-law Emperor Ferdinand that his brother and heir, Archduke Francis Charles, should renounce his place in the Habsburg succession so that his young son Francis should become Emperor, taking the name Francis Joseph. Grand Duchess Vladimir may well have seen herself as another Archduchess Sophie.

However, the very thought of marrying their beloved eldest daughter off to Grand Duke Boris shocked the Tsar and Tsarina to the core. How, Alexandra wrote in fury to her husband, could 'a pure fresh girl eighteen years his junior' possibly marry a half-worn, blasé man of thirty-eight and live in a house in which 'many a woman had "shared" his life!!'

Not in the least surprised at this rejection of her son, the tenacious Grand Duchess considered such alternative plans as were feasible. In the lively conversations which dominated her *soirées* and dinner parties, criticism of and at length outright scorn for the Tsar and Tsarina were

Royal group at Windsor Castle, 17 November 1907. *Seated, left to right*:
King Edward VII; Infanta Isabella of Spain; Princess Henry of
Battenberg; Grand Duchess Vladimir of Russia; Queen Amelia of
Portugal; the Duchess of Aosta; Princess John of Saxony. *Standing, left to
right*: the Princess Royal, Duchess of Fife; the Duke of Connaught;
Maud, Queen of Norway, holding her son, Crown Prince Olav;
William II, German Emperor; the Princess of Wales; Princess Patricia
of Connaught; the Prince of Wales; Alfonso XIII, King of Spain;
Augusta Victoria, German Empress; Prince Arthur of Connaught;
Queen Alexandra; Grand Duke Vladimir of Russia; Victoria Eugenia,
Queen of Spain; the Duchess of Connaught; Prince John of Saxony

Beatrice, Infanta de Orleans y Bourbon

Grand Duke and Duchess Cyril of Russia with their daughters, Princesses Kira and Marie

The Russian imperial family, *c.*1914. *Seated, left to right*: Grand Duchess Olga; Tsar Nicholas II; Grand Duchess Anastasia; Tsarevich Alexis; Grand Duchess Tatiana. *Standing*: Grand Duchess Marie; Tsarina Alexandra

Grand Duke Michael of Russia, brother of
Tsar Nicholas II

Marie Feodorovna, Dowager Empress of
Russia

King George V and Queen Mary

King Gustav V of Sweden

Queen Marie of Roumania

Grand Duke and Duchess Cyril of Russia (*both seated*), his brothers and his sister, 1920. *From left*: Princess Nicholas of Greece; Grand Dukes Andrew and Boris

Grand Duchess Cyril of Russia, arriving on SS *Paris* at New York, December 1924. Always self-conscious about her teeth, she rarely smiled for the camera

Grand Duchess Cyril of Russia, *c*.1927

Grand Duke and Duchess Cyril of Russia and Grand Duke Vladimir
(*left*), breakfasting at Ker Argonid, 1933

Grand Duchess Cyril of Russia, *c.*1935

Grand Duchess Kira of Russia and Prince Louis Ferdinand of Germany
at Doorn on their wedding day, 2 May 1938, with the Prince's
grandfather, William II, former German Emperor

recurrent themes. Out of this bitterness, and her unwavering ambition for her sons, came talk of conspiracy. In January 1917, while society still rejoiced over Rasputin's murder, the moderate conservative President of the Duma, Michael Rodzianko, was sent an urgent invitation to lunch at the Vladimir Palace.

After they had eaten, the Grand Duchess began to talk of the general state of affairs, of the government's incompetence, of certain ministers and the Empress. She mentioned the latter by name, becoming more and more excited, dwelling on her malign influence and interference in everything, and said she was driving the country to destruction; that she was the cause of the danger which threatened the Tsar and the rest of the imperial family; 'that such conditions could no longer be tolerated; that things must be changed, something done, removed, destroyed . . .' When Rodzianko asked precisely what she meant by 'removed', the Grand Duchess replied that 'She must be annihilated.' 'Who?' 'The Empress'. At this, Rodzianko, mindful of the proprieties, asked her to allow him to treat this conversation as if it had never taken place, in order to excuse him from being compelled by his oath of allegiance as President of the Duma to wait at once on His Imperial Majesty and report to him that the Grand Duchess had declared to him that the Empress must be annihilated.

Nevertheless, details escaped somehow. Everyone in Petrograd, it was said, knew that four regiments of the guard were to make a night march on Tsarskoe-Selo and seize the imperial family. The Tsarina was to suffer the customary fate of unwanted or inconvenient consorts, and would be confined in a convent, and the Tsar would be forced to abdicate in favour of his son, with the popular Grand Duke Nicholas as regent.

The British and French ambassadors to Petrograd, Buchanan and Maurice Paléologue, were accredited to the Tsar and thus had no right to speak on matters affecting Russian imperial policy. But they were begged on all sides, as representing Russia's allies, to use their position to plead with the Tsar to appoint a government acceptable to the Duma. In view of the fact that nothing else could save Russia as an ally, they reluctantly agreed to do so, but their carefully-chosen words failed to move him.

By now, the forces of revolution were gaining momentum. Shortly after Ducky's return to Russia from Roumania, early in the new year, disorder broke out in the capital. There were strikes in the industrial areas and factory towns, workers' demonstrations, riots and food shortages, mutinies in the barracks, violence against officers, and murders of the police.

As one of the few senior members of the Romanov family who saw events at first hand during those traumatic weeks and lived long enough to commit them to posterity, Grand Duke Cyril's account is particularly important. In his view, the mob and revolutionary soldiers in the capital were not particularly antagonistic to the Tsar; all they wanted was food, an end to the war, and distribution of land and wealth. 'Much of what they shouted and of what was told them by agents of the revolution they did not even understand. They had picked up slogans and repeated them like parrots. The people as such were not disloyal to the Emperor, as were those in the Ministries and in his entourage. As for the troops in the capital, they had enough of everything and far too little to do.'[9]

News of the revolution spread across Europe in haphazard fashion, much of it exaggerated. Among the first telegrams to come back to Petrograd from alarmed European courts was one from Queen Marie of Roumania,

asking for information about her sister Grand Duchess
Cyril, whom she was mistakenly informed had been
captured.

Those in command of the troops at Petrograd, asserted
Cyril, had lost their heads completely. One of his Naval
Guard battalions was responsible for protecting the
imperial family at Tsarskoe-Selo, but the situation had
become so dangerous in the capital that he ordered them
to rejoin the rest of the Guards as these were almost the
only loyal troops still left which could be relied on to keep
order if matters deteriorated even further. Military
authorities in the capital gave contradictory orders from
day to day; mob rule, hooliganism, and chaos reigned,
with continuous shooting by day and night, and with rival
gangs looting shops, private houses, and hotels. With
nobody to take a firm hand against such behaviour, the
gangs became even bolder.

One day, an armed rabble broke into the courtyard of
Ducky's and Cyril's house. The leaders demanded to see
Cyril, and he walked out to them expecting the worst. He
was relieved when they asked him politely to lend them
his car as they wanted to go to the Duma. He told them
that they could take it as long as they did not smash it,
whereupon they all burst out cheering and called on him
to lead them. 'I think there was something in that
demand which the masses felt very strongly,' he recalled.
'They felt the absence of leadership, they wanted guidance of some kind and were then still harmless enough.'[10]

If only, he remarked later, some leadership could have
been found at that time, the situation might have been
saved. It was precisely this vacuum which the Bolshevik
party saw and later exploited. They provided leadership
and a new direction, although both led the country to
tyranny and bloodshed on a hitherto undreamed-of scale.

On another occasion, an officer of the naval guards
came to Cyril in a state of alarm. The sailors, he said, had

locked up their officers and trouble was brewing in the barracks. Cyril hurried off immediately and spoke to his men, who were in an ugly temper. He managed to restore order, although it was an unpleasant experience for him. Despite the prevailing revolution and anarchy, Cyril felt the men were still loyal to him. They had volunteered to provide him, Ducky and their family with a guard, and despite the chaotic state of affairs they were not molested. Every night, friends called in to see how they were, and to discuss the situation. They did so at great risk to life and limb, for anyone who went into the city streets at night was liable to be fired at indiscriminately.

At length, anarchy became so prevalent that the government issued an appeal to all troops and their commanders to show their allegiance by marching to the Duma and declaring their loyalty, so as to try and re-establish some kind of order amid the chaos. The government hoped that if the troops could be got to carry out its emergency measures in the capital, normal conditions might yet be established and the 'rule of gangster-dom checked for good and all'.

The government's decree put Cyril in a very awkward position. He was commander of the naval guards, which constituted one of the military contingents of the capital. It therefore applied to his men as it did to all other troops, and also to him as their commander. He had to decide whether to obey that order and lead his men to the Duma, or whether to leave his men leaderless in this dangerous situation by resigning, and thus let them drift into revolution with the rest. Hitherto he had succeeded in preserving loyalty and discipline among them; they appeared to be the only loyal and reliable troops left in the capital. It had not been an easy task to preserve them from 'the contamination of the revolutionary disease'. To deprive them of leadership at such a time would have added to the disaster. Cyril saw it as part of his duty to try and calm things in the capital by every means at his disposal, even at cost to his personal pride, in order that the Tsar might safely return from the front.

As yet the government was not officially a revolutionary one, although it was leaning that way. But it was the last 'certain thing among the wreckage'. Therefore Cyril went to the naval barracks, still hoping 'that it would not be necessary to drink this bitter cup'. However, on arrival he saw that there was no alternative but to take them to the Duma. They wanted to be led. Accordingly, he marched to the Duma at the head of a battalion of naval guards. On their way they were fired at by some infantry soldiers, so he continued by car.

When he arrived at the Duma, he found the place in absolute pandemonium. It was like a bear garden. Soldiers with unbuttoned tunics and their caps pushed to the back of their heads were shouting themselves hoarse. Deputies were yelling at the tops of their voices. The place was in a state of chaos and confusion. Cigarette smoke filled the air, the place was in a filthy mess, and torn paper littered the floor. Meanwhile officers were driven up the stairs by their men with rifle butts. They were being bullied and insulted mercilessly. 'Liberalism and socialism expressed themselves in complete anarchy.'

Cyril spent the whole afternoon and evening in this painful atmosphere, guarded by his men. In the end a mining student came to his room and told him that a car was waiting to take him away. On their way back they were held up by an armed gang demanding to know who they were. The student shouted at them, 'Students, comrades!'[11] Whereupon they were allowed to pass. There were buildings on fire which lit up the night with their ghastly glare. An armed shouting rabble went through the streets. Machine-gun and rifle firing could be heard nearby.

After this chaotic interlude, noted Cyril, 'order was re-established and normal life resumed its course.'*

The French ambassador, Maurice Paléologue, noted with disdain in his diary that Grand Duke Cyril had not merely 'come out openly in favour of the revolution', but gone even further:

> Forgetting the oath of fealty, and the office of aide-de-camp which bound him to the Emperor, he went off about one o'clock this afternoon to make obeisance to popular rule. In his naval captain's uniform he was seen leading the marines of the Guard, whose commander he is, and placing their services at the disposal of the mob![12]

When Cyril reached home he found Ducky in a state of great anxiety after his long absence. She thought that all was over with him. Yet never once did she waver from her support for Cyril, or her conviction that he was doing the right thing. To Missy, she wrote shortly after the revolution 'a brave and noble letter, just as one would imagine she would write'.[13] She emphasized their sympathy with the movement for obtaining a freer government, and added that the new government were their friends; but they feared that as 'the people' were taking the upper hand, and the new masters had to make concessions to 'the mob', they would probably be sacrificed for the sake of keeping momentary peace at home.

As feared, the rule of the Romanov dynasty was at the end of the road. On 16 March 1917, Tsar Nicholas II abdicated in his own name and in that of his son and heir, Alexis, who could not be parted from his parents and

---

*At no point in his memoirs does Cyril refer categorically to his march to the Tauride Palace in order to pledge his allegiance to the provisional government.

family on grounds of ill-health. He appointed his brother
Michael to succeed him, but Michael refused to accept
the imperial crown. When the troops at the front were
told, they refused to believe it at first. They had been
confident of eventual victory, especially as an offensive
had been fixed for April which they hoped would lead
them to the long-expected triumph for which they had
suffered so cruelly for the past two and a half years.

To Cyril, it was the saddest moment of his life.
Thereafter, he wrote, 'all seemed futile and hopeless.
Hitherto there had been hope.'[14] He handed in his
resignation, and with a heavy heart went to address his
men. He told them that in his position he could not
continue to lead them. He exhorted them to remain loyal
to their country, to honour the virtues of discipline, and
to obey their superiors; for twenty years, he had been
with them, and this was the hardest day in his life. When
they heard of the Tsar's abdication, he recalled, there
were tears in their eyes. Then they rushed up to him,
seized him in their arms, and lifted him on their
shoulders, saying, 'Where you are, sir, we will be.'

Some of them continued to guard him, Ducky and the
girls, for the remainder of their time at St Petersburg. On
Easter Saturday, a delegation of sailors came to their
house and insisted on them coming with them to their
chapel in the barracks to attend the liturgy of Easter
night with them. They showed them where to stand in the
church.

Ducky and Cyril could still count on the friendship of
Sir George and Lady Buchanan, although the position of
the British Ambassador and his wife was now somewhat
precarious. In his first interview with Miliukov, newly-
appointed minister of foreign affairs in the provisional
government, Sir George was told rather brusquely to have
no further communication with the imperial family. To
this, he replied that he would certainly not drop old

friends who had been kind to him, adding that if there was trouble, he would offer the protection of the British embassy to the Grand Duchess Cyril, as she was a British princess by birth and entitled to any help he could give her. Miliukov received this statement coldly.

Lady Buchanan continued to visit Ducky and took her out in the embassy carriage to visit her English nurse, who was ill in hospital. After hearing of this Miliukov sent for Sir George again, and told him sternly that he could not allow this fraternization to continue. In certain quarters, he said, people believed that the British ambassador was plotting a counter-revolution with members of the imperial family, and he would have to ask for his recall to London, as if an angry crowd was to attack the embassy, he could not be held responsible.

It was a hard decision to take, but Sir George had to consider not only his personal safety and that of his wife and daughter, but also the fact that the embassy was British property, and that Britain had officially recognized the provisional government in Russia. After a long discussion, Lady Buchanan wrote to Ducky, and told her what had happened. She was comforted by the most gracious of replies:

> I quite understand, and thank you both for all your
> niceness. Of course you must not think of coming
> to see me, if it can be misinterpreted. It is hard to
> be accused of being *vieux regime* when all one's
> sufferings are due to mismanagement. Fondest
> love, and I hope we will meet again in happier
> days.[15]

Unhappily, the Buchanans' motives were misunderstood. Distrusted by the new British Prime Minister, David Lloyd George, who saw in him the personification of a diplomat of the old school and therefore a reactionary, he was also blamed by others for not having done enough to prevent Russia's slide into revolution. Ducky wrote rather unfairly to Missy that he had deserted her in her hour of need, and had refused to help her.

By April, even her tenacious spirit was close to despair. 'Neither pride, nor hope, nor money, nor future,' she told Missy, 'and the dear past blotted out by the frightful present; nothing is left, nothing!'[16] To add to her complications, she was expecting another child in the late summer.

In declaring their allegiance to the provisional government, Cyril had almost certainly saved the lives of himself and his family. Because of the revolutionary chaos in St Petersburg, his only alternative would have been to risk death as a hero and martyr in the name of the imperial cause, and dragging his wife and children down with him to share the same fate. This, however, was not the view of their other relatives in Russia. As far as they were concerned, Grand Duke Cyril had sworn an oath of allegiance to the Tsar, who alone could release him from it. They regarded him as a coward and a traitor, and never forgave him.

Suspicion and jealousy undoubtedly played their part in the contempt in which he and Ducky were held thereafter. None of the Grand Dukes from the other branches of the family could forget that only the ailing Tsarevich and his Uncle Michael had stood between Cyril and the succession, or the plotting behind closed palace doors with which Grand Duchess Vladimir had been rightly or wrongly credited. In his haste to swear allegiance to the provisional government the day before news of Tsar Nicholas's abdication, perhaps they thought he was intending to ingratiate himself with the ministers and put himself forward as their first choice of a more democratic, more accountable Tsar.

At the same time, they probably cursed their own

indecisiveness when only one of their number was prepared to make a stand. For as long as they could
remember, they had enjoyed an existence of imperial
luxury on which the more sordid aspects of the outside
world had barely impinged. Suddenly, the Romanovs'
own world was in shreds. Uncertainty and revolutionary
chaos confronted them, and they were totally at a loss as
to what to do. Beneath their contempt of Cyril and his
so-called cowardice, perhaps, lurked a sneaking admiration for his courage. Having served in the Russian navy,
he appreciated the importance of making instant de-
cisions when danger loomed – be it under enemy fire on
board ship, or when revolutionary mobs stood within a
stone's throw of his palace and family.

Order of a kind descended over the city again after
Easter, but as Cyril realized with hindsight, it was merely
the calm before the storm. He and Ducky guessed that it
would be courting disaster to remain in the capital, and
they decided to settle in Finland for a time. They had
been invited to move to Borgo, a small town close to the
Haiko estate. This belonged to the von Etter family, who
had been close friends for a long time and had frequently
entertained them there. Marie and Kira had been there in
July 1914 when Cyril and Ducky had to go to
St Petersburg for receptions organized in honour of
Poincare, President of the French Republic, then visiting
Russia; the girls were still staying when war was declared,
and their parents had some difficulty in getting them
home, as the trains were full of troops. In the summer of
1916 Ducky had visited Haiko again with the girls, and
they were later joined by her mother-in-law. The girls
spent most of their time outdoors bathing, while Ducky
visited the small military hospital for the wounded which
had been organized on the estate. As ever, she found
relaxation in her painting.

There was no need to contemplate anything as undignified as flight from their country. Kerensky, minister for war, was sympathetic to their application to leave, and he ensured that no obstacles were placed in their way when it came to issuing them with the documentation necessary for their departure.

CHAPTER *9*

'Three long years'

Ducky and Cyril left St Petersburg in June 1917. Their palace was not ransacked by revolutionary soldiers, as were so many others, but when they were granted permission to go, they were forbidden to take anything of value with them. All that went with them were such clothes as they could carry, and as much family jewellery as they could conceal about themselves.

According to legend, Cyril fled with his heavily-pregnant wife across the frozen Gulf of Finland, with the Bolsheviks in hot pursuit. Such a story is worthy of Hollywood legend, but bears little relation to the facts. In the first place, his leg injury and poor circulation would have made the feat physically impossible. Secondly, had the four of them attempted to run with revolutionaries at their heels, they would have almost certainly been captured, imprisoned, and eventually shot. Moreover, the Gulf of Finland would not have frozen over during summer.

Some thirty years later Kira, by then Princess Louis Ferdinand of Prussia, wife of the head of the house of Hohenzollern, recalled the flight she had made as a girl of seven with her parents:

We left Russia, St Petersburg, in the early summer of 1917 during the first months of the Provisional Government of Kerensky. It was our plan to spend some months in Finland, then still a part of Russia, at the country house of friends. Here we hoped to tide over safely the period of unrest and

danger threatening in the city. At that time no one
believed in a general upheaval. It was thought that
Kerensky's government could consolidate itself and
be able to restore order.

We reached Finland safely, travelling by train. I
do not remember much of the journey except that
for the first time there were no royal trappings to
it, i.e. red carpets, special comforts, etc. We had
travel passes signed by the government; these were
respected and we were not molested on the way.[1]

On their arrival at Borgo, the family went at once to
Haiko Manor, accompanied by some of the servants. The
rest were installed in a house at Borgo rented by Cyril,
and his equerry, K.N. Hartong, also took up his quarters
there. Once they were installed, Ducky wrote to Missy to
reassure them where they were, but that although safe
she was suffering from severe cramp in her legs and could
hardly stand. 'Her despair at the last events in Russia can
find no expression,'[2] Missy remarked sadly.

After spending a fortnight at Haiko, the family moved
to Borgo, where they stayed till the end of August. On 30
August Ducky gave birth to a son, whom they named
Vladimir. Once she was well enough to move, they
accepted an invitation from the von Etter family and
returned to Haiko, hoping that they would be safer there.

Vladimir was christened at Haiko on 18 September.
The Very Revd Protopresbyter Alexander Dernov, head
of the court clergy and Dean of the Cathedrals of the
Winter Palace, Petrograd, and of the Anunciation in the
Kremlin of Moscow, came to conduct the ceremony. He
was assisted by V.I. Ilyinsky, Psalmist of the Cathedral of
SS Peter and Paul in Petrograd. Godparents by proxy
were Grand Duchess Marie and Grand Duke Boris. The
christening was attended by a few Russian exiles and
some of their Finnish friends.

Life in Finland for the family was severe. Like the story of Ducky being carried across the Gulf, it has been subject to exaggeration, with accounts of Cyril devotedly sawing the door and window frames of their tiny wooden log cabin into logs in order to keep them warm throughout the depths of winter. Nevertheless they did suffer from food and fuel shortages, as well as the anxiety of not knowing what had become of the rest of the family.

Again, according to Kira:

> The few months we expected to stay in Finland
> dragged out into three long years. During those
> years we experienced the hardship of bitter cold,
> hunger, privations of every sort, not to mention the
> constant danger of being murdered by the Reds
> and the terrible sadness of the political
> developments.
>   In spite of all the misery of that first period of
> our life in exile we kept many memories of Finland
> – of the beauty of the summers, the forests, the
> Gulf; of good friends and the many pastimes with
> which we filled the long, dreary winter months.[3]

Hearing of their plight, Lady Buchanan sent them a case of Red Cross stores, clothes for the children, tinned milk, butter, cereals and jam. Yet the only thanks she received came in a letter from the English nurse, coldly acknowledging the gift's arrival. A little later, Cyril gave an interview to members of the press, in which he said that Sir George and Lady Buchanan had turned their backs on them after the revolution. In vain did Lady Buchanan wait for a personal message from the Grand Duchess who had been her friend for so long.

Sir George was unfairly blamed by the Romanovs for 'guilt by default' for abandoning Tsar Nicholas and his family to their fate. The Foreign Office in London ini-

tially offered asylum to the former ruler, and then withdrew their invitation on the grounds of political
expediency. Britain's helpless Ambassador in St
Petersburg was forced into accepting responsibility for
his country's refusal to offer hospitality, and later gallantly falsifying his memoirs to this effect. Not until 1932,
eight years after his death, did his daughter reveal that
the Foreign Office had threatened to terminate his pension if he dared to tell the truth.[4]

One of Cyril's sailors from Russia found his way to the
family, and also brought them provisions, including wine
and cakes. He told them that he looked upon the revolution as 'a farce, which would end sadly'.

Even at Haiko, Ducky and Cyril could not feel
secure. The Baltic fleet was stationed in Helsingfors and
though the officers were still theoretically in command,
their authority had suffered considerably from revolutionary disintegration in which the Sailors' Revolutionary Committee played a great part. Finland herself
was on the point of seceding from Russia, and the
discontent of national elements against communist
influence was growing. The 'white' movement against
the 'reds' which was to lead to civil war had already
started.

One day a group of sailors appeared unexpectedly on
the estate, declaring that they had orders to search the
house. Ducky and Cyril had already heard unconfirmed
reports of most of the other Romanovs being placed
under arrest, and they prepared themselves for the worst.
With the children, they moved to the second floor of the
house, and endured an exceptionally uncomfortable few
hours. Yet no arrest or even search followed. It later
appeared that when the sailors were told the house was
inhabited by Grand Duke Cyril and his family, they
decided not to proceed with their search but left. One of
them had served under Cyril's command on *Oleg*. As he

had been very popular with the crew, the man persuaded the others not to disturb him.

Towards the end of the year, civil war broke out in Finland. The country had been united with Sweden from the early middle ages until seized by Russia in 1809, when it was created a Grand Duchy within the Russian empire, and guaranteed constitutional government. The Tsar of Russia's titles therefore included that of Grand Duke of Finland. Finnish autonomy was respected until the end of the century, when a policy of Russification was inaugurated, leading to suspension of the constitution in 1903. After the Russian revolution of 1905 the Finns regained their autonomy, and next year they were granted the power to elect a Diet chosen by universal suffrage. Further repression began in 1910, and the Finns took advantage of the Bolshevik revolution to proclaim independence. This led to civil war the next year between the Conservative groups and Germans, led by General Charles Mannerheim, a former officer of the Russian imperial army, or the 'whites', against an alliance of radical socialists, communists and Bolsheviks, or 'reds'.

The first hostilities took place near Haiko, and the family heard gunfire all too frequently. Living on the edge of a war zone and with the onset of winter, obtaining essential supplies of food became even more difficult for a while. Several landowners were captured and shot by the reds, and a number of Finnish whites came and took refuge in the house. When the reds were informed, the whites made good their escape.

In February 1918, a band of about fifteen Finnish reds appeared near the house, and asked if there were any arms hidden in the rooms. Three of them made a brief search of the ground floor. The family were all on the second floor, but none of the reds went up there. They behaved with the utmost respect, and the way in which they put their questions suggested that they were under orders not to touch anybody in Haiko, and to be particularly polite towards the Grand Duke and Duchess.

Though Cyril's naval connections apparently gave his wife and children a degree of respect and therefore safety not accorded to the rest of his kinsmen, they were nevertheless in a precarious position. They were almost cut off from the rest of the world, and only heard extraordinary, often contradictory rumours about their relations. At the end of February, Cyril heard news from Helsingfors that the French government was making enquiries as to their safety, and whether it was necessary to make arrangements for their evacuation. A few days later, word arrived that King Gustav of Sweden was extending a similar offer of help, through the Swedish Legation.

Grateful as Ducky and Cyril were for such consideration, they declined. To accept, they believed, would look like desertion, and they thought that the Bolsheviks' tenuous grip on power would soon be loosened. Nevertheless it had been tempting to say yes; to be looking after a family of three children, one a babe in arms, in such trying conditions, was not one they endured by choice.

From Stockholm, a letter (24 January 1918) from the Crown Princess of Sweden, formerly Princess Margaret of Connaught, to Lady Egerton, wife of the Duke of Connaught's Comptroller, throws some light on the plight of Russians in general and her cousins in particular:

> . . . I feel so sorry for all Russians, I know several
> very nice ones here who feel so ashamed of their
> country. One I like very much is a C(ounte)ss
> Orloff Davidoff who is a typical Russian, short,
> stout, magnificent pearls, ugly clothes, a deep
> voice and very downright, a little like Aunt Marie
> in manner, she manages to get news from Russia
> some how & told me last night she had heard that

the Empress Minny is better but she has been very
ill a long time & has apparently grown so old. No
wonder! This Css Orloff brought me a letter from
Ducky asking me to be kind to her, she is here
with her only child & P(rince)ss Lieven who is
expecting her first baby & whose husband is the
Russian Red X's representative here in Sweden.
Curiously enough they have not sent him flying yet
altho' belonging to l'ancien regime. Ducky & Kyrill
are staying with a Mme Etter in Finland, Ducky at
last got a son last September, rather late in the day
poor thing. Kyrill we hear has to go about & buy
his own food at the market . . . [5]

In the spring, a German squadron arrived in Hango,
and later in Helsingfors; a German ultimatum demanded
the withdrawal of the Russian Baltic fleet to Kronstadt;
the German Iron Division under command of General
von der Goltz entered Hango; and Mannerheim achieved
final victory over the reds. The civil war in Finland was
over, and the threat of enemy action receded.

Ducky and Cyril must have looked on it with mixed
feelings, for it amounted to temporary German triumph.
So did the treaty of Brest-Litovsk, signed in March
between the Bolshevik government and the central
powers, by which Russia surrendered or recognized the
independence of Poland, Finland, the Baltic provinces,
and the Ukraine.

It made little difference, as far as food shortages were
concerned. Another letter that summer (28 July 1918)
from the Crown Princess of Sweden to Lady Egerton
made it evident that their plight was not yet over:

. . . I had a letter from Ducky from Finland two
days ago begging me to send her some baby food
for her 8 months old boy, they can get nothing to

give him, doesn't it sound rather awful. I shall do
my best to help her of course.[6]

Homesickness, shortages, cold weather and boredom
hung over them like a pall. Kira wrote (28 May 1918) to
Queen Marie of Roumania:

> How I wish I could see you. Here it is quite cold
> though it ought to be summer. Boy is so sweet.
> When he is hungry and Nana is preparing his
> lunch, the tears simply stream down his cheeks
> with hunger. We go for long walks and hunt for
> mushrooms in the woods. There are many wild
> flowers in bloom. Each Friday we go to the cinema.
> On Saturday evenings we have games . . . I often
> wonder if we will ever go away from here. We are
> getting so dreadfully homesick but I suppose we
> are better off here. When there is no more sugar I
> think we will miss it very much. Our lessons keep
> us occupied, otherwise we are rather bored
> sometimes . . . [7]

By this time Kerensky's moderate provisional
government had been overthrown by Lenin and his
followers. Civil war still raged throughout Russia, and
Ducky and Cyril were not content to look on impassively
while the country they loved tore itself apart, or to wait
helplessly while the Bolshevik menace threatened the
rest of the free world. British troops had been sent to
Russia before the treaty of Brest-Litovsk, partly to create
an eastern front against the Central Powers, and partly to
prevent stores of ammunition from falling into German
hands. The British government and military circles were
bitter that Russia pulled out of the war in March 1918,
and believed that the Bolsheviks had thus declared
themselves traitors to the Allied cause. It was felt,

especially in the War Office, that Britain should help the anti-Bolshevik Russians to destroy Lenin and his regime. There was widespread revulsion at the news that the former Tsar, his wife and children, had all been butchered in captivity at Ekaterinburg in July. Such feelings of horror and a comprehension of the situation were intensified in September when Bolshevik troops broke into the British embassy in Petrograd to search the building, and killed the naval attaché, Captain Cromie.

After the armistice in November, war-weary British forces had no stomach for further fighting. It was a view with which Lloyd George wholeheartedly concurred, but not the secretary of state for war, Winston Churchill. The latter was determined that Allied forces should march on Moscow and stamp out the foul disease of Bolshevism before it could spread any further.

Lloyd George set himself firmly against the idea of intervention. He believed that the one certain way of establishing Bolshevik hegemony in Russia was to try and suppress it with foreign troops; to send British soldiers to shoot down the reds would be to create great sympathy for Lenin's supporters in Britain itself. Meanwhile he compromised by inviting the warring Russian factions to conclude a truce and send a delegation to the peace conference in France (an invitation which met with a frosty response on all sides, and brought Lloyd George criticism at Westminster for his apparent readiness to fraternize with an extremist regime), while still sending limited armaments to the whites. If Russia was really anti-Bolshevik, he insisted, a supply of equipment would enable it to redeem itself; if it was pro-Bolshevik, then it was none of Britain's business to interfere with its internal affairs. Launching a new war against Lenin's Russia would be the direct road to bankruptcy and Bolshevism in Britain.[8]

From Finland, Ducky and Cyril railed against Lloyd

George's policy. Although the inspiration, it must be assumed, was to a certain extent that of Cyril, Ducky it was who appealed passionately from Borgo, in a sixteen-page letter (29 January 1919), to her cousin King George V:

Though neither Kirill nor I have the slightest wish or intention of playing a political part, I have been asked to lay before you once more the feelings of all true Russians & to give you an exact picture of the desperate conditions in Petersburg. I undertook to do so, having the possibility of writing to you unofficially in the hope that it may accelerate the sending of help so urgently needed. That this cry for help should remain unanswered we still refuse to believe in spite of the news that has just reached us that England, ignoring France's willingness to assist us, has definitely refused all help to her former true ally, Russia. Also the news that England has invited the Bolsheviks to the peace conference is considered by Russia a crime such as history has never known. A crime before which the abomination & baseness of the Brest-Litovsk peace (an everlasting shame to both the sides that signed it, and which logically ended in bringing about Germany's downfall) pales into insignificance, being a crime towards the world at large.

Is it possible that England does not see that she is courting the same disaster that overtook Germany, in her attempts at recognising the Bolsheviks as a respectable and legitimate government? Is it possible that great political men such as England has at the head of her government fail to realise that the bolsheviks do not represent the democracy of Russia and that they are not

socialist, even in the remotest sense of the word;
that they are nothing but the scum of the earth
profiting of a momentary madness to maintain
their power by a reign of terror against which all
humanity & civilisation cry aloud. This proposal of
dealing with the Bolsheviks will inevitably lead to
one of the largest political mistakes ever made by
any country, as only we who have lived, through &
under their regime are fearfully & terribly
competent to judge – in a way that none of you,
not even the greatest politician amongst you, can
hope to be. Excuse this plain language, but those
who have been through this have a right to speak.

This letter is to ask for help to destroy the
source itself from which this contamination of
bolshevism spreads over the world. In the coming
struggle for freedom from the bolsheviks, struggle
which even Lloyd George will not be able to stem
by temporising with them, Petersburg remains the
chief object of military operations. In spite of this,
General Judenitch, the head of the Russian
military formations on the coast of the Finnish
gulf, has not been able to equip his army, nor has
he received an answer to his appeal to the Allies,
sent end of December. Yet his forces will be called
on to play a most important part when our
northern, eastern, & southern armies will be
approaching Petersburg, as the only means of
preventing the retreating bolsheviks from invading
Finland & the Baltic provinces.

As all the above mentioned armies, with Admiral
Kolchak at the head, are receiving ample support
from the Allies, officially or unofficially, we implore
the same help for this western army without which
its further formation becomes hardly possible.
Every week's delay makes the position more

serious. Petersburg is dying of hunger, and though
this army which is now in formation is
geographically & therefore strategically in the most
advantageous position for the decisive blow to the
stronghold of Bolshevism, we dare not deal it
without an ample supply of food for the starving
population. If you could but send us sufficient food
transports to feed this army & the population of
Petersburg for a few weeks, the military operations
could start immediately, even though the army
were insufficiently equipped in other respects, very
little assistance being feared. Independent of
nationality, Russians, Finns & Balts are ready, all
to march together against the enemies of humanity
& civilisation, but without food we can do nothing.
Petersburg at the present moment has reached the
limit of human endurance, the population reduced
to some seven hundred thousand souls who are
dying of starvation & want. The remaining
supplies of food are entirely in the hands of the
bolsheviks & not allowed to reach any of the
population not belonging to the bolshevik
organisations – all the bourgeoisie and higher
classes & a great part of the working classes, not
employed by the bolsheviks are literally dying daily
by thousands for want of food clothing & warmth.
Their lodgings are taken from them – all former
officers & officials are thrown into prison and
forced into bolshevik service by drastic measures
such as the shooting of their entire families, wives
& children. The cruelties increase daily the crimes
& horrors committed are such that they cannot be
put down on paper. Is England who has ever been
the first to raise an indignant protest against
cruelty oppression & tyranny, now going to
remain, not only an impassive onlooker, but by her

trying to recognise the bolsheviks as a government,
a partaker in the most heinous & monstrous
enterprise that ever the world has known.

Please forgive anything in this letter which may
sound uncourteous or presumptuous and
remember that I am only the mouthpiece of real
Russia, trying to make itself heard in the midst of
the world's tumult. Not the voice of one or another
political party – but the voice of all the parties
united in one great endeavour to save their country
from anarchy & murder.[9]

It was a letter which the King received 'with feelings of
the deepest concern', as his reply (13 March 1919) from
Buckingham Palace confessed:

. . . together with my Ministers I have given careful
consideration to the points which it raised.

There is no truth in the news which reached you
– that while France was willing, England refused to
assist Russia. On the contrary, we have been
anxious to do our utmost to help, so long as we
could be certain that we were giving assistance to
the right people.

Equally is it untrue that England wished the
Bolsheviks to be represented at the Peace
Conference. We fully recognise who, and what they
are. We are appalled at and outraged by their
revolting crimes, and realise that they are daily
becoming an international danger – a danger from
which it behoves us to defend our own land.

Our desire and intention is to send food and
munitions to those who are resisting the
Bolsheviks, and before your letter was written,
effect had been given, to a certain degree, to carry
out those intentions. For, on the 1st December,

four light cruisers and six destroyers arrived at
Libau with a large consignment of arms, some of
which were supplied to Esthonia and to the
Latvian Government at Libau, and the light
cruisers actively assisted in the operations against
the Bolsheviks.

By this time a force of light cruisers and
destroyers must have reached Libau with more war
material, including 20,000 rifles, six 6" howitzers,
twelve 18-pounder guns and 20 motor lorries. No
assistance has been asked for from the Admiralty
by General Judenitch.

In December, when he was in Finland, an
unofficial application for arms and ammunition to
assist the formation of a new Russian Army was
made to the War Office, but no requests came
through diplomatic channels. However, the above
mentioned supply of munitions was despatched,
and arrangements have also been made for an
early supply of coal to the Esthonian Government.

I recognise and sympathise profoundly with the
terrible condition into which the people at
Petersburg and Moscow have been brought under
Bolshevik domination, and also can understand
what you say – that if Petersburg were occupied,
order restored and the starving population
supplied with food and clothing, an important step
would have been taken in the regeneration of
Russia.

There is unfortunately a serious obstacle in the
deficiency of ships, which increases the difficulty in
carrying out our wishes.

To this end I am exerting my utmost
endeavours, but please remember that nothing can
be done except through concerted action of the
Entente powers which, in itself, constitutes a

serious element of delay, and I must add that the lack of any united action of the Russian people themselves, adds to the complexity of a problem which seems to be almost insoluble.[10]

To which Ducky replied (22 July):

Once more I have been asked by our leading men to give you a brief account of the present situation here. The kindness with which you answered my last letter enables me to do so. We are fully aware of the reasons & difficulties of the allied governments which are inducing them to withdraw from us their help at the most urgent moment. We see however that our representatives have failed to give you the impression of the imminent danger such a course is creating, and of the European disaster it is conjuring up.

The present situation is as follows. Admiral Kolchak's retreat, caused by the want of ammunition etc. on which it had counted, has endangered General Denikin's successful advance. His right flank is exposed to the full forces which the bolsheviks have been enabled to withdraw from the Eastern front & which they are now throwing against him & our moth-eaten army. Should Donikin in consequence meet with the slightest defeat, then now Finland, the last buffer state between Northern Europe & bolshevism, must unavoidably succumb. To prevent such a contingency all our energies must be concentrated on the immediate taking & retaining of St Petersburg by our North-Western army. This can only be done with the help of Finland. All questions as to the participation of Finland in this undertaking have been clearly settled & accepted

between General Judenitch & General
Mannerheim. General Mannerheim can march any
moment if he receives from England the
declaration that she will give Finland her full
moral & material support without which he is not
in a position to propose such a step to his
government though he is backed by the whole of
his country. Finland is naturally too weak to
support such an undertaking on her own.
Therefore we ask that England should insist on
Finland's immediate advance on Petersburg.
Should, however, the English government find it
impossible for her own reasons to put this pressure
on the present Finnish ministry, she could achieve
the same result by fully supporting General
Judenitch, by supplying him with all necessary
material support with which to supply Finland. As
Gen. Mannerheim & Judenitch are working in
complete understanding & similar interests of their
countries, it is of the greatest urgency that the
English government should not lose a moment in
doing this & that Petersburg should be taken in
the next few weeks before the bolsheviks have time
to concentrate their forces, taken from the Eastern
& Southern fronts (which they have already started
doing) to throw them over Finland and the
Scandinavian countries, by which England herself
would be threatened. We press the full particulars
of this bolshevik plan.

Great Russia with Petersburg & Moscow, have
so reached the limit of human endurance, under
the despotic rule of the bolsheviks, that they are
now ready even to accept help & salvation at the
hands of Germany. German agents are already
fully at work all over Russia offering with true
German precision, point by point, all help for

present & future – in fact are preparing themselves
an alliance with Russia, which, if the Allies
continue in their present unreliable politics
towards us, will eventually be accepted by all anti-
bolshevik parties independent of their political
views & feelings. Such a result would ultimately
enable Germany to throw off & annul the
obligations of the treaty of Versailles.

Russia, once liberated from the bolsheviks & more
or less in working order has sufficient food supplies
to feed herself & Germany for years to come, thereby
rendering any future blockade of Germany
ineffective. I have been asked to express the
necessity that all the above mentioned negotiations
with Gen. Mannerheim & his ministry should be
kept absolutely secret. The present moment is of
vital importance especially from all points of view of
the League of Nations. Bolshevism puts an end to all
true democracy, not to talk of the unrealizable
socialistic ideal. In asking for assistance against
bolshevism one cannot sufficiently insist on the fact
that the allied governments are not asked to help
retrograde imperialism but are fighting for the
people & for true democracy independent of their
future form of government. It is all important that
such countries which still have sound governments
themselves should not reach that stage of dissolution
which hands over the power to the rabble as
happened in Russia.

General Gough at the head of the English
military mission here is fully acquainted with the
military & political situation in Finland & has
inspired all parties here with full confidence.[11]

With this, the correspondence apparently closed.
Ducky had to concede that, much as her cousin deplored

the Bolsheviks and feared the consequences that their
ascendancy in Russia might have for western Europe, he
was powerless to act further.*

On 2 August 1919 the government granted the family
permission to stay in Finland until 1 January the following year. Cyril did not renew their application to remain
there any longer, and left a few weeks later. Though the
country had been most hospitable to them, they were
tired of living in the provincial town of Borgo, especially
under such trying and primitive conditions. Travelling
through Germany, they stayed two days in Berlin with
Ducky's sister Sandra, met their mother Marie in
Munich, and all of them travelled together to Zurich.

The Dowager Duchess of Coburg had lost almost
everything, apart from her jewellery. Most of her Russian
relations had been murdered, and Germany, with whom
her full sympathies had been during the war, was van-
quished. Her Russian income was in Bolshevik hands.
She now lived in a shabby annex of the Hotel Dolder
Grand, the Waldhaus, Zurich, on a small pension. Since
Ducky had last seen her, she had lost weight. She was
bent almost double and walked with uncertainty, her
once plump hands now thin and trembling. Yet still she
had not lost her spirit or her domineering character. She
blamed Missy for her role in the war, and bitterly accused
her of rejoicing over the devastating peace terms forced
on Germany at the Versailles conference.

---

*The main commanders of the white forces met with mixed fortunes.
General Mannerheim retired from public life after the civil war, but
entered Finnish politics in 1931, a career which culminated in his
serving as President, 1944–46. General Judenitch fled to exile in
France and died in 1933. Admiral Kolchak, regarded as the whites'
standard-bearer, was captured by the Bolsheviks and shot in 1920.

The changes wrought on Ducky's mother-in-law were also pitiful. Grand Duchess Vladimir had last been heard of at her Red Cross hospital in the Caucasus shortly before the revolution. Stranded, with Grand Duke Andrew and his mistress Matilde, shortly to be his wife, she made her way to the port of Novorossisk on the Black Sea, the white Russians putting a train at her disposal. An Italian ship brought the party, and many other refugees, to Constantinople, where they boarded a ship for Venice. When the family met her there they no longer recognized the once tall, superbly-dressed leader of Russian society. Though only in her mid-fifties she was bowed and broken, lean, and white-haired. She went to recuperate at the spa of Contrexeville, but her health and spirits completely shattered by the ordeal, she died in September, a few weeks later.

Grand Duchess Marie's health was likewise failing, and she died suddenly at Zurich in October. According to legend, she collapsed on receiving a letter addressed bluntly to 'Frau Coburg'. Her body was taken back to Coburg for burial. Ducky and Baby Bee joined Sandra for the ceremony, but Missy discovered to her dismay that she could not return to Germany, even for a private family occasion of this nature, without provoking an international incident.

The main legacy from the Dowager Duchess to her daughters consisted of the jewels which were to provide a ready source of badly-needed income for Ducky in the future. When Missy's daughter Elisabetha married Prince George of Greece in February 1921, Missy and Nando gave her a chain of diamonds with a huge sapphire pendant, which they had purchased from Ducky.

All the same, Missy continued to provide financial support for her sister and the family. For a time, it had to be sent through Queen Mary, whom she had told (10 March 1920) that

I have had no more news from her for several
months although I have also tried to send her
things through our Roumanian Minister in
Holland.[12]

After leaving Finland, Ducky and Cyril divided their
time between Château Fabron, Nice, and the Palais
Edinburg, Coburg, left to Ducky by her mother. The
latter had been their main home before they were permitted to return to Russia in 1909. Everything here reminded
them of the happiest days of their life together, those first
years of marriage. The interior decoration had not been
changed at all; every piece of furniture was in exactly the
same place as it had been twenty years before. In an
uncertain world which, for Ducky and Cyril, had altered
almost beyond recognition in those two tumultuous
decades, it was a comfort to find that one or two things, at
least, were still the same.

CHAPTER *10*

'Magnificently resigned and uncomplaining'

Many of the Romanovs had perished in the last three or four years. Ducky's mother-in-law was one of the few to die of natural causes, although her health had undoubtedly been broken by her experiences after the revolution. The Tsar, Tsarina, and their children had been executed by firing squad; Grand Duke Michael, who had been named as his brother's successor in the deed of abdication but declined the crown of the disintegrating empire, had been captured and shot, as had Cyril's uncle Grand Duke Paul. Ella, the widow of Grand Duke Serge, had met her death after being thrown down a mineshaft. Grand Duke Nicholas, the Dowager Tsarina and her daughters Grand Duchesses Xenia and Olga, and Ducky and Cyril themselves were among the few fortunate enough to escape to safety in exile.

Yet Ducky found it hard to adjust to a new and very different existence. As Meriel Buchanan later remarked, 'after years of unhappiness she had married the man she loved, and, having at last got all she wanted, saw it destroyed, and herself faced a future of despair and bitterness, an exile in poverty and humiliation.' In time, she learnt to adapt herself to circumstances; but even then she was never quite able to resign herself to the loss of power and position.[1]

According to gossip, while they lived at Coburg, Cyril indulged his passions for hunting, golf, motor cars, political intrigue, and beautiful women. His circle of followers was said to be small and isolated. Even his most loyal publicist in Munich, Nicholas Snessarev, often had trouble getting to see him, since Ducky and their friends formed a barrier to keep out any unwanted visitors. It was maintained that she managed to obtain from abroad some of the funds needed for Cyril's political activities, and that she collected for the National Socialist German Workers' (later Nazi) Party, of which she was apparently an even more fervent supporter than her husband. Max Scheubner-Richter, an early supporter of Adolf Hitler, and his wife Mathilde became close personal friends. The Grand Duchess Cyril and Mathilde would sometimes watch the stormtroopers drilling in a Munich suburb, and attend Nazi meetings and parades together.*

What was the extent of Ducky's supposed Nazi partisanship? It has been suggested, though without any convincing evidence, that she was simply attracted by their anti-communism and anti-Semitism (largely as many of the leading Bolsheviks had Jewish blood), and that she contributed some of her remaining valuables to be sold to raise funds for them. It was only to be expected that any political movement which appeared to offer salvation from Europe for the Bolsheviks would provoke interest, if not active support, on her part, particularly since in the inter-war period most people of royal or noble birth were mistakenly assumed to be either pro-Nazi, or at least deeply fearful of Bolshevism, of which the most obvious opponents by the end of the decade were the Fascist powers. Her sister Sandra also believed for a while in Hitler's vision of a regenerated Germany.

*There was no properly constituted National Socialist Party yet in Bavaria, but the state had witnessed a Communist revolution, and any Russian refugee would naturally favour any fanatically anti-Bolshevik party.

Was Ducky convinced that support for the movement could further Cyril's imperial aspirations, and also assist in a restoration of the German monarchy? Did she cultivate right-wing politicians, help to finance Hitler's fledgling party, and did she and Cyril visit a German day rally in Coburg in 1922? Such assertions have been made but never proved. Yet allegations of her making vast donations to Nazi funds are undoubtedly false, as she could simply not afford to.

In the summer of 1924, Cyril proclaimed himself guardian of the imperial throne. Ducky recognized how vital this was in helping him to restore his self-confidence, shattered after a nervous breakdown the previous year. For a time, he had been unable to cross the street without holding her hand, or sleep unless she sat up next to him. With this grand if empty gesture, he – if not she as well – had a purpose in life again. It is questionable whether she really believed that they would be able to return to Russia one day at the head of a restored Romanov empire, but with the unsettled state of Europe during the 1920s they still clung to the hope.

In September, he issued a signed manifesto proclaiming his assumption of the imperial title. The 4,000-word statement, which began with the words, 'There are no limits to the sufferings of the Russian people', regretted the dreadful famine which had befallen the country, and the lack of international aid that could be expected from the United States of America or elsewhere until a law-abiding government was established in the Fatherland. 'Therefore let the mass of people rise together with the army and recall its lawful Tsar.' As there was no doubt that Tsar Nicholas, the Tsarina, and all their children, and the next in succession, Grand Duke Michael, had all been murdered, and as the Russian laws of succession did not permit the imperial throne to remain vacant, he was therefore taking for himself the title of Tsar of all the Russias.

His action was bitterly contested by most of the aristocratic survivors of the revolution. They pointed out that his uncle Grand Duke Nicholas, former Commander-in-Chief of the Russian army, had a stronger claim, in addition to his war record, as regards seniority and age. His young cousin, Grand Duke Dmitri Paulovich, had been involved in Rasputin's murder, and was thus regarded as more deserving of gratitude. Meanwhile the Dowager Empress, from her retreat at Hvidore in Denmark, declared that there was no such dynastic issue to consider as her son, daughter-in-law and grand-children were still alive. Yet though she continued to talk of her family as if this was the case, Grand Duchess Olga was convinced that deep in her heart her mother 'had steeled herself to accept the truth some years before her death'.[2]

Most other members of the family refused to recognize him. Added to everything else was their lingering resentment that Cyril acted with treasonable haste in declaring his loyalty (or yielding, as they put it) to the provisional government, before Tsar Nicholas's abdi-cation. As a member of the Romanov family, the Grand Duke had sworn an oath of allegiance to his sovereign and cousin, who alone could release him from it.

Among Cyril's critics – and surely the one whose pronouncements disturbed him the least – was the woman who claimed to be Grand Duchess Anastasia. She maintained that she was the sole surviving daughter of Tsar Nicholas II, and had been wounded at Ekaterinburg but made good her escape, and was in fact the only survivor of the massacre that had exterminated the rest of her immediate family. Doubtless under pressure from those who supported her claim, she denounced Cyril as a 'pretender' and announced that under Romanov law he should be tried for high treason in time of war. If he wanted the old laws back, he should begin by hanging himself.[3] Ducky did not escape her wrath either; she was contemptuously referred to by Anna as 'that Coburg'. 'If he and his wife come into my parents' place,' said Anna, 'then there is no God!'[4] Though they differed on many things, Ducky and Cyril were united with most of the family on one matter: namely that 'Anastasia' was an impostor. They steadfastly refused to have anything to do with her, let alone meet her.

Grand Duke Nicholas had already assumed the leadership of all groups of exiled Russians which had been formed from the evacuated units of General Wrangel's army. The Supreme Monarchist Council claimed the leadership of all monarchist organizations in exile. This opposition owed its existence to widespread belief among the Russian emigrés in the possibility of further armed intervention against Bolshevism, and they thought that Grand Duke Nicholas, in his capacity as former Commander-in-Chief, was the only one with sufficient authority to place himself at the head of such a movement. This was but a faint hope and Cyril, knowing as much, firmly believed that in the long run the majority would come round to his point of view, and that the patriotic cause which he had initiated would grow and develop.

He was so sure of his claim that he had sought no approval from other members of the family prior to making his proclamation. Although Russia was firmly in the grip of Bolshevism, he maintained that it was his duty to show a continuation of imperial authority and to provide a rallying point for the Russian emigrés.

Simultaneously, Cyril elevated their three children from prince and princesses to grand ducal status. This ran counter to a Romanov family statute whereby only sons and grandsons of sovereigns in the male descent bore the grand ducal style. Nonetheless he declared his son and heir Grand Duke Vladimir Kirillovich of Russia, and his daughters Grand Duchess Marie and Grand Duchess Kira. As self-proclaimed Tsar, he could maintain that the statute made by his grandfather was now null and void. Every day he rose at sunrise, and withdrew into his study to issue orders, offer imperial thanks, sign promotions, and send out imperial directives. Since the recipients of many of these were local taxi drivers, waiters and even titled gigolos, they were of little significance.[5]

Inevitably his actions caused a split in the promonarchist ranks. Both Grand Dukes had their devoted adherents; Cyril was regarded as more liberal and less reactionary in outlook, and he had been closer in line of descent than Nicholas. His memoirs (completed after his death by Grand Duke Vladimir) suggested that the majority were on his side, and that in every country where Russian exiles had settled, groups were formed to keep in close contact with him.

Less biased sources suggest that the truth was rather different, and that most of the Russian emigrés, especially from the colonies in London and Paris, were against Cyril's claims. Very few Russian exiles recognized him as Tsar, and treated them just as any other Russian Grand Duke and Duchess.

Few of the family, apart from Cyril's brothers Boris and Andrew, supported him. Fond as she was of Ducky, her sister-in-law Helen, married to Prince Nicholas of Greece, was critical of his attitude. Several of Queen Victoria's granddaughters, notably Queen Marie of Roumania and the late Empress Alexandra, had been widely recognized as determined women and wives, stronger than their gentle, weak-willed husbands, and there was no reason to suppose that Grand Duchess Cyril was much different from her sister or cousin. On the contrary, she was widely 'credited with all the ambition which Queen Victoria imparted to her granddaughters'.[6] Many of their royal relations in Europe who did not know them very well recalled Cyril as handsome, charming and elegant, but thought Ducky a very strong character, rather stiff and proud, even military in her manners. She certainly did nothing to dispel the impression that her personal ambition and pride had spurred her husband on to making his claims, and that she was responsible for keeping pressure on him to play the part of Tsar.

The rivalry which had characterized the Vladimirs manifested itself again in his wish to compete with Grand Duke Nicholas, and she undoubtedly played her part in kindling the rival spirit. At any rate, she was only too happy to give others the impression that she believed they would eventually return to Russia and claim their rightful inheritance. At a banquet one night, Cyril roared with laughter at some amusing remark. Ducky admonished him gently at this lapse of dignity. 'Remember, Cyril, you will be Emperor one day!' she exclaimed in full hearing of the other guests.

Nicholas's supporters claimed that Cyril had no right to the throne as he was born before his mother had embraced the Orthodox faith, rumours that he had abdicated his right to the succession while they were still in Russia, and so forth. But in order to consolidate his position and to determine once and for all his own right and that of his descendants to the Russian throne, he was assuming the imperial title which belonged to him by right of primogeniture, and in accordance with the fundamental laws of the Russian empire regarding the succession.

In October 1924, the United States of America press devoted considerable space to the imminent arrival of Grand Duchess Cyril of Russia. Her motives for visiting the New World gave rise to much excited rumour and some confusion. Initially it was stated that she was coming to give informal lectures in New York, in connection with work for Russian relief, under the patronage of

Mrs Henry P. Loomis, a member of the advisory committee of the Monday Opera Supper Club, an organization devoted to collecting funds for the starving of
Russia. Such rumours were quickly denied, and it was
announced that, according to another committee
member, she was coming 'simply in recognition of the
efforts made by the club to aid her suffering compatriots
in Europe'.[7]

It was soon followed by a lengthy denunciation of
Cyril's actions, and in effect an outspoken attack on
virtually everything he had ever done during his life.

Taking as its cue a rumour that he was about to sail for
New York with his aide-de-camp, General Sipoupski, to
confer with American capitalists who were anxious to
bring about the restoration of the Russian monarchy in
order to resume stable trade relations between America
and Russia, the press wished to remind its readers of 'the
peculiar position of this particular action of the imperial
family'. It asserted among other things that the Soviet
government secretly approved and was fostering Cyril's
role as self-proclaimed Tsar in order to promote dissen-
sion in the monarchist ranks and render united action
impossible, as most of the family strongly supported
Grand Duke Nicholas. A former secret agent of Tsarist
Russia, Colonel Balashev, was credited with being the
instigator of his pretensions. The Colonel had apparently
defected to the Bolshevik cause during the revolution, but
later changed his mind and went to Paris in 1923,
declaring to Cyril that he wished to work again for the
imperial cause. Cyril had already, stated the article,
earned himself great unpopularity (as well as the nick-
name 'Cyril Egalité') for taking an active part in the
intrigues leading to the downfall of Tsar Nicholas II and
giving enthusiastic support to the revolutionary junta,
making a public profession of his republican doctrines
and belief, and confession of how he had always opposed

the policies of his sovereign and cousin. Demanding to be
known henceforth as 'Citizen Cyril Romanov', he was left
unmolested at Petrograd at a time when all his other
relations were being rounded up and imprisoned, most of
them to suffer eventual execution. When the Communist
regime took over from the Provisional government, he
'became alarmed for his own safety, for which he has
always had a great regard'. While his wife was helping to
nurse the wounded and cholera-stricken at Jassy, he
abandoned the luxurious home which he had arranged
for himself in Finland, made his way across the frontier
into Sweden and thence to Paris. As a result he was
received coldly by the French government, and 'he was
given plainly to understand that his presence would not
be welcome in Great Britain'.

Following this attack was an ill-informed condemnation of his service in the Russo-Japanese war, during
which it was said that he had suffered nothing more than
shock, but bitterly resented that he was not the first to be
rescued from the waves, on the grounds that he was the
principal personage aboard. He had resigned his
command and 'under the pretext of peremptory orders of
his physicians retired to the south of France to convalesce'. Nor did he take any active part in the war, being
the only member of the house of Romanov to fail to do his
duty in this respect.[8]

Any hopes, such as they were, that Cyril might have
had of visiting the United States must have been dashed
instantly by this damaging and largely inaccurate dia-
tribe.

Nonetheless, on 29 November Ducky set sail from
Le Havre on board the steamer *Paris*, accompanied by two
ladies-in-waiting, Madame Makarov, widow of Admiral
Makarov who had lost his life on board *Petropavlovsk* in
1904, and Countess Orlov. Ahead of her went a message
to the women of America: 'Tell them of my joy at meeting

them and how happy I will be to thank them for all they have done for us.'[9] 'The possible future Czarina', as she was tactfully referred to by journalists, arrived on 6 December at New York, under conditions of strict security. To forestall the possibility of Bolshevist attack, the acting police commissioner had provided ten motor-cycle policemen to escort her to her hotel, the Waldorf-Astoria. Another fifteen patrolmen were posted on the pier.

From her suite on board *Paris*, the Grand Duchess emphatically denied that there was any political motive in her visit to the States. She said that it was purely social and had been decided on before her husband issued his manifesto proclaiming himself Tsar. A report that he intended to come to America himself, she said, was untrue, and a rumour that a visa to his passport had been refused him, she maintained, was absolutely without foundation. When asked if she thought the old Russian nobility would return to power in the near future, she neatly sidestepped the question: 'I am here simply as a grateful woman to thank the American people for their kindness and I do not wish to talk of political matters at all.'[10]

In a statement prepared for reporters, she wished 'to invoke the courtesy of the newspapers in publishing a complete and unequivocal denial' of all reports that her visit was for political purposes, to help restore the Russian monarchy, or to sell property.

Reporters were fascinated to have a member of European royalty in their midst, and described her appearance and dress in great detail, as she posed on the deck for photographers. After noting her close-fitting blue costume and coat of turquoise blue trimmed with sable, her large black felt hat and suede slippers, they then turned their attention to the three pearl rings on the fingers of her right hand, pearl earrings, jade bracelet and a dagger pin of Russian amethyst. She spoke her native language – English – with only a slight Russian accent, they observed, and that she was 'tall, rather thin and has keen gray eyes, with fair hair turning gray. She is younger and not so attractive looking as her sister, the Queen of Rumania.'[11]

Rumours soon surfaced that Tsar Nicholas II had made large personal investments in the United States, said to be about $60,000,000, held in the National City Bank. The Grand Duchess said she did not even know that any sum existed, preferring to make diplomatic comments on the country.

'I am immensely surprised at the size of the place,' she replied when asked for her impressions of New York. 'And everything is in such beautiful order. Your traffic police are perfectly amazing and those motorcycle men who have been accompanying me do the most extraordinary things in getting through traffic. And the Broadway lights! There is nothing like them in the world. They make your nights a charming and a beautiful thing.' At a performance of Schubert's *The Student Prince of Heidelberg*, which she and her party attended at the Jolson Theatre, 'the singing was as good as any I have heard. You Americans do things up in a most extraordinary way.' As for the police, she was quite 'in love' with them; 'they are a fine body of men.'[12]

Yet it was only a matter of time before she was drawn on political questions. In an interview at the Waldorf on 9 December, when asked if she believed that the Russians wanted a monarchy, or whether they were satisfied with the new regime, she replied that 'every sane person knows they are dissatisfied with the present government. Just read their statistics and you will find out why.' The rest of her interview was taken up with more innocuous subjects. 'Shopping? They don't give me time for that.' She was introduced to crossword puzzles, and admitted later that she had tried three but not solved one. She was quoted as saying that she enjoyed this method of 'word-juggling' very much, and that crosswords might catch on in Russia: 'The whole world is a puzzle just now.' Did she think that New Yorkers really rushed around as much as they were said to? 'Yes, I do, and I enjoy seeing it. I like to see people who get a move on.' And she expressed her support of careers for women, adding that Russian women were 'independent to a large degree, and very serious'.[13]

The Grand Duchess arrived in Washington on 11 December to a marked absence of official honours, as the State Department refused to accord any honours apart from a small guard of uniformed policemen. The wife of a former member of the city administration had telephoned the Department to request that a Russian royalist flag be sent to the Grand Duchess's hotel, the New Willard, and draped over the chair to be used when she received 'the homage of her admirers'. Officials replied firmly that the enquirer evidently misjudged the intricate diplomatic requirements of the occasion. It was stated that she would be guest of honour at several functions given by Washington society leaders, including a ball held in the interest of Russian relief, but no engagement had been made for her presentation to President Coolidge. There would be no complications over the propriety of her social reception by the first lady of the land, as Mrs Coolidge had left Washington that morning for an absence of several days. Whether her departure was by coincidence or design, to avoid being upstaged, was left to the citizens of Washington to decide for themselves.

Denunciations in the press of Grand Duke Cyril's imperial pretensions and support for Grand Duke Nicholas, probably instigated by Russian emigrés in America, overshadowed this part of the visit. They were

possibly instrumental in Washington's official policy of
giving their visitor no more than a lukewarm reception,
but she put a brave face on it and refused to allow herself
to be provoked into any statements that might be con-
strued as retaliation. Her secretary, Captain George
Djamjarov, was asked rather bluntly whether Grand
Duke Cyril had been popular with the Romanovs. He
shrugged his shoulders, remarking non-committally that
'a Grand Duke is always a Grand Duke, you know'.

A *New York Times* editorial suggested that talk of a
Russian monarchist restoration, even if it took no sub-
stance beyond argument between rival candidates for the
Romanov throne, would help Communist prestige at a
time when matters were not going well for Communism
in other European countries. The present regime, it
suggested, could 'always be bolstered up effectively by
inviting the Russian people to consider the alternative of
the Czar and the landlords coming back'. Despite the
repression of elementary civic rights and liberties of the
Russian proletariat, the Soviet leaders preferred 'to util-
ize the fear of Czarism for the maintenance of their own
unimpaired dictatorship . . . The fact that the Russian
people today has less work, less food, and less education
than it had under the Czar will be overridden by the fear
of a relapse into still worse conditions and the prospect of
reprisals.'[14] The inference was that the Grand Duchess's
visit to the United States could not mask the divisions
between both rival Tsars, one of whom was her husband,
and that although by crossing the Atlantic she had done
nothing to prejudice the imperial cause, the publicity her
appearance had brought benefited none but the present
Soviet regime.

In Washington, opinion was even more scathing. 'Soft
murmurs of adoration, happy bleatings,' said the press,
greeted the Grand Duchess who 'was on exhibition to
those worthy of the vision', while the jaundiced grumbled

that she was not much of an ex-potentate, and that the
Grand Duke bore a name 'which makes some of us think
of Offenbach and champagne and all the lost delights of
our frivolous ancestors'.

Shortly before her departure on 16 December, the
Grand Duchess diplomatically told journalists at a farewell interview in the Waldorf Astoria that she was sorry
to leave; 'Americans everywhere have been so kind to
me.' When asked how American society compared with
that of Europe, she said that she found them 'extra-
ordinarily well-informed'. As she left on the French liner
France, it was remarked that she looked much better in
health and spirits than she had on her arrival. The
diversion and excitement of New York and Washington
society, if not unanimously friendly, had evidently done
her good.

She arrived in Paris on 23 December, still singing her
hosts' praises. 'If everybody copied the Americans'
upright, common sense,' she declared, 'there would be
less trouble in the world. It was my first visit to the
United States, but I hope to go again. I think my
American friends will continue to help Russian refugees
as they have done in the past.' She denied that she had
brought back any funds; she had not asked for any. All
she returned with were thanks for the reception she
received; 'everywhere I went I found great sympathy for
Russia and the hope of seeing her in order again.' To a
question that she had said America needed royalty:
'America needs nothing. She is getting along beautifully.
Prohibition? It didn't interfere with me.'[15]

It did not take some disgruntled sections of the American public long to start asking awkward questions once
she had left. Her hosts at the Monday Opera Supper Club
were pressed to issue a statement denying that any funds
had been expended in connection with the Grand Duchess's visit. The steamship company and management of

the Waldorf likewise had to deny publicly that they had supplied her and her suite with any free entertainment or accommodation.

On 25 November 1925 Ducky's elder daughter, Marie, was married in Coburg to Charles, Hereditary Prince of Leiningen. The first ceremony was celebrated according to Orthodox rites in their private chapel in the Palais Edinburg. The vestments and decorations of this chapel were presented to the Duchess of Edinburgh by her father, and originally belonged to the moveable military chapel attached to his headquarters during the Russo-Turkish war of 1878. After the Orthodox ceremony, a Lutheran marriage was celebrated in the local church.

Soon after their daughter's wedding, Ducky and Cyril purchased the house that was to become their permanent base in France two years later. This was Ker Argonid, at the little fishing village of St Briac-sur-Mer, an unpretentious Breton stone building erected by a retired captain in the 1880s, with granite masonry and stained pine woodwork. With her gift for colour and decoration, Ducky soon transformed it, supervising the necessary alterations and organizing the removal of their furniture from the flat in Paris which they had kept on during the war. Devoted to flowers and gardening, she wasted no time in taming the wilderness outside. At last she could devote herself to her talent for painting, illuminating old books and Bibles, and selling her pictures of flowers. The money this brought in helped her to keep the household going, and to pay for the education of their children.

Sinister motives were attributed to their settling at St Briac. Shortly after Cyril's proclamation in 1924, the Bavarian Communists called for his expulsion, as the republic could not permit an alleged court to function within its borders. 'Unemployed royalty, it appears, has become a serious problem in Bavaria,' the *New York Times* reported.[16] Ferdinand, former Tsar of Bulgaria, had returned to his native Coburg, although he could hardly be accused of creating any problems, leading the quiet life of a wealthy country squire. As Germany had established friendly relations with the government at Moscow, the Communists suggested that Grand Duke Cyril should take his court 'to some place where monarchies are more popular'. The Government rejected this demand, arguing that his behaviour did not warrant their denying him the right of asylum. There was no truth in assertions that the Bavarian ministers had asked him to leave after he refused to sign a statement promising to desist from further political activity.

All the same, Cyril and Ducky could not be blamed for moving, if it meant that their presence in Bavaria was an embarrassment. St Briac was in the process of becoming home to a colony of White Russians and retired English people, many of them former officers on half-pay. Moreover, the climate was mild. Ducky had always suffered in cold weather, and with his war injuries, Cyril was a martyr to circulatory trouble. Both required somewhere warmer to live.

There were several English families at Dinard, and in the summer, cosmopolitan visitors brought gaiety and entertainment to the place. Cyril played golf nearly every day, he and Ducky joined in picnics and excursions, and became part of the social life of the community, going out to play bridge, and organizing theatricals and *tableaux vivants*. During the winter months they would invite large numbers of local guests to their parties, joining in the games. It was, however, considered good manners to let Cyril and Ducky win at their favourite game of 'Murder', and any youngster from the community who dared to beat them was left in no doubt as to their displeasure. Yet it all made for a more lively existence than the drudgery of post-war Coburg.

However, Ducky still lived in constant dread that Vladimir might be kidnapped by their enemies. She was reluctant to let him out of her sight, and refused to send him to school but instead engaged a private tutor for him. She would not let him learn a trade or profession, and insisted on bringing him up as if he was to inherit the position and wealth of his ancestors. He was offered a scholarship to Winchester School, but Ducky vetoed the plan, probably out of fears for his safety, but perhaps also – it has been said – out of fear that the experience might transform him into an Englishman.[17]

Missy came to visit the family, watching with concern and some disbelief while Cyril acted the part of the Tsar, while Ducky worked in the garden, and worried about their future. To a friend, the Queen wrote sadly about her sister who looked so badly lined, overworked, and too tired to think about her personal appearance: 'No home, no fortune . . . no hope – trying to keep things together, to make both ends meet, with a family accustomed to live in utmost luxury.'[18] Cyril would be seen regularly on the golf course in Brittany in his favourite London-made hat, which he wore till the day he died.

To King George V, Missy wrote (29 November 1925) that 'Ducky is in very sad circumstances, but both she and Kirill are magnificently resigned & uncomplaining, bearing nobly almost unbearable misfortunes.'[19]

Earlier that year, Kira had written dejectedly (19 June 1925) to Queen Marie:

Mummie is as usual dreadfully overworked; it never stops, only gets more and more. If at least she had some capable secretary but she hasn't found one and done most of the work herself. Her tiny room is simply littered with papers and

letters; as she says she soon won't be able to turn
around in it . . . She looks so tired and worried
again and when she came back from America she
was looking decidedly fresh and not so
harassed . . .[20]

After Ducky's return from a visit to Missy three years
later, however, Kira was more optimistic. After telling her
aunt (12 August 1927) how much good it had done her
mother and how she hoped 'this may be the beginning of
more visits in the future', she went on to sing the praises
of their Breton retreat:

This is a little hidden-away corner, full of peace
and quiet which I think you would like as much as
we do. It has been the source of much trouble and
work but now certainly repays it.[21]

A young Englishman, Edward Voules, later recalled
spending a short holiday at Dinard at about this time. A
Russian wedding was about to take place and his woman
friend had been invited to the wedding breakfast afterwards. She obtained an invitation for him, but when he
arrived he could find no card on the table bearing his
name. Seeing this forlorn stranger slinking around, the
Grand Duchess Cyril called him to her side to ask what
was the problem. When he explained, she was so excited
to find 'a raw young man from England' in her midst that
she instructed a waiter to squeeze in an additional chair
for him next to her so that he could give her news of her
native land.

As a result of this chance meeting, he came to know
Ducky, her husband and the two younger children well.
While there he was invited to other parties and frequently
danced with Kira. They kept in touch and he would see
them when they came over to London to stay at Kings

Cottage, Chiswick, a grace and favour residence lease-loaned principally to Baby Bee and her husband by King George V. Sometimes Kira and Vladimir stayed there without their parents, and all three would attend parties in the city together.

As for the Grand Duke and Duchess themselves, his memories were of 'a quiet, austere man who spoke very little, leaving conversation to his vivacious and ebullient wife who was as talkative as was said to be her sister Queen Marie'.

The Grand Duke appeared to lead a very unobtrusive life though he was generally polite and courteous to everybody, and both were known to have only modest means on which to live. This, Voules noticed, was immediately evident from his first meeting at the wedding luncheon. Ducky was wearing a ring with one gigantic pearl, and remarked to him that this was the next piece of jewellery for which she was looking for a buyer in order to help meet their living expenses.[22]

By 1926, such hopes as Russian monarchists in exile still nursed of the former Tsar, his family and brother still being alive, had largely evaporated. Nicholas Sokolov, an examining magistrate appointed by Admiral Kolchak, was in charge of investigations into the Romanovs' fate. In the course of several visits to Brittany, he acquainted Ducky and Cyril (neither of whom had ever really doubted the official version of events) with the facts in great detail. This added weight to Cyril's belief that he was by right of primogeniture the senior surviving member of the imperial house, and consequently head of the dynasty.

On 13 October 1928 the grand matriarch of the family, Dowager Empress Marie, died at her Danish retreat of Hvidore, at the age of eighty. She was buried at Roskilde

Cathedral, last resting place of the Kings of Denmark. Cyril travelled by train from Paris to Copenhagen for her funeral, staying as the guest of her nephew King Christian X and Queen Alexandrine. He was received with all the honours due to the head of the imperial house of Russia, many of whose other surviving members gathered together for the first time since the revolution.

For a brief moment the splendid pageantry of imperial Russia was relived, as tributes were accorded to the last surviving crowned head of the once mighty Romanov empire. Every royal house in Europe was represented, and Russian exiles in their hundreds flocked to Denmark. As the Empress's youngest daughter, Grand Duchess Olga, commented ruefully, it was ironic that so many members of the family hardly gave a thought to her while she was still alive, but came to the funeral as if to salve their consciences, even Cyril, 'who should have had the sense to stay away'.[23] It must have been irksome for her when the Danish press feted 'Tsar Kyrill, Keeper of the Throne', taking it upon himself to act the leader, leaving his seat in the church at the funeral to conduct Danish royalty to their seats.

Three months later, on 5 January 1929, Grand Duke Nicholas died at Antibes, on the Côte d'Azur. Aged seventy-two, he had been in failing health for some time, and unable to play any part in public affairs. Now Cyril was beyond doubt the senior surviving member of the family, and his position as Tsar-in-exile unassailable – for what it was worth.

Ducky and Cyril had never had a close relationship with Grand Duke Nicholas, and they had never met in exile. Cyril had fully recognized Nicholas's authority as the eldest male member of the family and did not belittle the services which he had rendered Russia as a soldier, but Cyril was officially head of the dynasty by 'virtue of the Fundamental laws', and resented Nicholas's refusal to support his claim. Cyril had made attempts to establish friendly relations with his late kinsman, but to no avail.

With the death of Nicholas, the military organizations were deprived of their natural leader. The obvious course for them to take, maintained Cyril, would be to recognize his authority. This they did not do. Not that the 'legitimist cause' suffered, according to Vladimir; on the contrary, it grew and gained in strength from year to year. Legitimist groups were organized in every country throughout the world where Russians had settled. Cyril's general secretariat, as he grandly called it, kept in touch with all of these, and he was well informed about everything that happened among the Russian emigrés. As the main protagonists of the White Russian movement left the political arena, and chances of foreign intervention diminished, so did the hopes of Cyril and his legitimist movement grow. As Vladimir optimistically put it, the soundness of his father's forecasts 'was continually being confirmed by the trend of political events, which assured the success of his cause'.[24]

This was the version of events according to Cyril's memoirs, as completed posthumously by his son. Other sources, however, make it evident that most of the Russian emigrés, particularly in Paris and London, had little sympathy for his cause, and regarded him as just another Russian Grand Duke with absurdly-inflated ambitions that took no account of circumstances in the outside world – and one who could never be forgiven for his treason in swearing allegiance to the provisional government before the last Tsar's abdication.

In the spring of 1929 Cyril transferred his general secretariat to St Briac, and resumed his Coburg habit of hearing reports from the secretary-general every morning.

His activities were detailed in Grand Duke Alexander's

memoirs, published four years later. St Briac, wrote
Alexander, was 'the phantom capital of an invisible
empire' where its Emperor lived a life of 'sustained
pathos'. His sovereignty had 'to be enforced solely by
mail' as 'each morning, the robust sunburned postman of
the village of St Briac appears on the threshold of the
improvised Imperial Palace, puffing and panting under
the weight of batches of letters which carry the stamps of
almost every country under the sun. The foreign representatives of the Shadow Emperor of Russia keep him
posted daily on the physical welfare and the morale of his
far-away subjects.'

One such letter from America suggested that 'a word or
two of Monarchical Encouragement would be greatly
appreciated by the impoverished Russian colony in
Harlem'. A former guards captain, now a dishwasher in a
self-service cafeteria in the Mid-West, was offended as he
had not been promoted though friends of his who had left
Russia as mere lieutenants had been made colonels.
Former Russian army officers in Manchuria, a Cossack in
Bolivia, and a general in India, all requested guidance on
the propriety and wisdom of protecting their new masters
from their rebellious subjects. A former Supreme Court
justice from Moscow, now a factory hand in Canada,
wished it to be understood in St Briac that a certain
young Russian employed in a Montreal bakery was 'a
very dangerous radical who should not be permitted to
return to Russia when the monarchy is restored.'[25]

In October 1930, Ducky and Cyril celebrated their
silver wedding. For twenty-five years, according to
Vladimir:

> they lived together with one heart and mind, and
> our family could well be an example to all. We
> adored our parents, and their love for us was
> infinite. All the hardships and bitterness we had to

endure in the years of exile were fully covered by
our mutual love. We were proud of our parents,
and the celebration of their Silver Wedding had a
special significance for all of us.[26]

Among guests at the celebrations, none was welcomed
more eagerly than Ducky's sister Sandra. Although Missy
had been the one to do more for Ducky in the last few
years, the bond between the latter and Sandra, who saw
her more often, had been just as strong.

They also received greetings from all parts of the
world, and many presents. On the evening of 8 October
they gave a large dinner, to which members of Cyril's
entourage, as well as their friends in St Briac, were
invited. After dinner, tableaux were staged, and much
appreciated. On Sunday, 12 October, representatives of
monarchist organizations arrived from Paris to present
loyal greetings. The visit was marked with a luncheon
party, and that evening a reception was held at Dinard in
the house of an American friend.

CHAPTER *11*

'She was our Conscience'

*F*ortunate were those royalties from deposed dynasties during the inter-war years who could resign themselves with good grace to living in humbler surroundings, with the pomp and circumstance of the late nineteenth century firmly a thing of the past. Perhaps none of them adapted better than the most theatrical monarch of his day, ex-Emperor William, who lived contentedly in Holland, developing a passion for archaeological research, chopping wood, and reading P.G. Wodehouse while he led what he described as the life of an English country gentleman. Well might he have agreed with the words of his cousin Princess Victoria of Hesse, now the widowed Marchioness of Milford Haven, speaking to Mary Ponsonby soon after her marriage: 'I dare say Royalty is nonsense and it may be better if it is swept away. But as long as it exists, we must have certain rules to guide us.'[1]

For the former German Emperor and King of Prussia and his family, and for many other once-exalted personages living in Europe during the thirties, the rules to guide them had indeed been swept away. Grand Duchess Cyril found it harder than most to adjust to the reality of a changing world. How much she really hankered for the glories of imperial St Petersburg is a matter of conjecture. Having to watch her household budget carefully, living modestly in Brittany, still afraid that she or her husband might fall prey to Bolshevik vengeance, certainly made for an uneasy and none too happy existence.

Nevertheless she could revel in such imperial splendour as she considered was due to her. In October 1932 she attended the wedding of Princess Sibylle of Saxe-Coburg Gotha and Prince Gustav Adolf, son of the Crown Prince of Sweden, at the church of St Moritz, Coburg. One of the last great royal weddings in Europe before the Second World War, it was witnessed by about one hundred and fifty guests. At presentations, the Ober-hofmarschall announced in Prussian drill-sergeant fashion: *'Die Kaiserin aller Russen, handkuessen und rueckwaerts treten!'*

This was too much for the punctured dignity of the notoriously touchy Ferdinand, ex-Tsar of Bulgaria. When the procession of royalty emerged from the church after-wards, the gouty septuagenarian did not hesitate to wield his stick – something between a sceptre and a field-marshal's baton – to brush aside anyone who dared to try and take precedence over him, *Die Kaiserin aller Russen* included. The spectacle of Grand Duchess Cyril glaring at him, expressing anger and dignified contempt at the same time, must have been an entertaining one for their fellow guests.

She tenaciously supported her husband in his self-proclaimed leadership as standard-bearer of the Rom-anovs, empty though she must have realized the cause was. As long as she had her family's undivided love and affection, all was well and good.

But around 1933, a blow fell. Throughout the years, Missy had visited her regularly at St Briac. The bond between the sisters had remained steadfast, and they had no secrets from each other. The Queen of Roumania had suffered several tribulations herself, not least the death of her husband King Ferdinand in 1927 and endless humili-ations heaped on her by her elder son, now King Carol, a trial she bore with resilience and dignity. In June 1933, she wrote cryptically to a friend that Ducky had 'had an overwhelming soulgrief which has shattered her concep-tion of life and humanity'.[2]

Missy and a few others – only the closest of her friends and relations – were told the truth, but sworn to secrecy. Cyril had had an affair with another woman. Infidelity on the part of a Russian Grand Duke was nothing new; by and large, the Romanovs had been notorious for their extra-marital affairs. However, Ducky's reaction to the news was one of anger and sadness, and from then on she avoided further physical contact with him. 'The most unforgiving of us all,' as Missy called her, from that day began to die 'by inches'.

Perhaps Ducky would have taken it less to heart had the relationship between them not been strained by outside circumstances. For a few years after the revolution, they nursed the forlorn hope that one day they would return to the throne of their ancestors in glory, by popular acclaim, and help to save their people from the Bolshevik menace. With this they had a common definite purpose in life, that bound them together despite a programme of independent travels. Ducky had been to the United States of America in 1924, and to the Coburg wedding in 1932, while Cyril had attended the Dowager Tsarina's funeral at Roskilde Cathedral in 1928 – on each occasion, they went alone. As the years passed and their health deteriorated, the hollowness of their existence added to the tedium of late middle-age. It only needed an affair such as this to cause a breakdown in their marriage.

There were a few family celebrations left to Ducky, however. On 30 August 1933 Vladimir's sixteenth birthday was celebrated. According to the fundamental laws of the Russian empire, this gave him the right of exercising all the prerogatives which belonged to him by virtue of his birth. Cyril issued a special manifesto addressed to the Russian people, and a circular letter to all the royal houses of Europe, informing them of his son and heir's majority. Grand Dukes Andrew and Dmitri, and several representatives of monarchist organizations, came from Paris to attend the ceremony, in the course of which he took a solemn oath. It was followed with a banquet given by Dmitri Paulovich in his honour. The affair must have seemed little more than a meaningless pantomime to contemporary observers, but it brought some brightness to Ducky's life – a life which by now had all too little colour or excitement.

In the following year, Ducky, Cyril, Kira and Vladimir were all invited by King George V and Queen Mary to attend the wedding of Princess Marina of Greece, daughter of Cyril's sister Helen, to Prince George, their youngest surviving son. The King had contemplated reviving the Dukedom of Edinburgh for George, and wrote to Missy to ask what her feelings would be on the subject. In the end, however, he conferred the Dukedom of Kent (vacant since the death of Queen Victoria's father in 1820) on George instead.

Ducky thanked Queen Mary profusely for the invitation (12 October 1934), although it was overshadowed by the assassination of King Alexander of Yugoslavia, her nephew by marriage, three days earlier:

> It is a very long time since anything has given
> us so much pleasure as this delightful invitation
> of yours . . . These last few days we have all been
> so dreadfully upset by the horrid death of Sandro
> of Serbia. The meeting of Missy and Mignon*
> in Paris was heartrending. What a terribly hard
> task poor kind Mignon has ahead of her. It must
> have caused you all great sorrow & anxiety –
> pray God it will give rise to no more
> complications.[3]

*Queen Marie of Yugoslavia, the King's widow.

On their arrival in England they stayed at Kew Green, and on the eve of the wedding there was a grand reception at Buckingham Palace. All the relatives, members of the diplomatic corps, and many others were invited. Among the diplomats was Ivan Maisky, the Soviet ambassador. It was the first occasion on which Cyril found himself near a representative of Soviet Russia and, noted Vladimir, 'no conversations passed between them'.

Vladimir was particularly impressed by his first experience of attending a court function on so vast a scale. Immediately before the reception he was presented by his parents to King George V, 'for whom I conceived an immense liking. There was something exceptionally attractive about the old King's manner.' Although he found the reception tiring, as he had to stand all the time, he went round the rooms with great interest and closely observed all the invited guests. He was introduced to so many friends and relations that he found it quite impossible to remember them all. There were several family dinners, but so many relatives gathered at each one that they did not seem like family affairs at all. One dinner was attended by no less than seventy-four members of royalty.

King George had always had a soft spot for his cousin, even since the happy, carefree days when they and Missy had played together and ridden their ponies on Malta. Perhaps a sense of guilt, at not having tried harder to bring Nicky, Alicky and their children into safe exile during the war, increased the sense of personal obligation he felt in providing Ducky and her family with the best hospitality he could.

For her part, Ducky was particularly pleased to be back in England. The times when she had to some extent shared her mother's resentment of their British relations, stirred up by the animosity of the Anglophobe German Empress Dona, were but a distant memory. Though relations with Grand Duchess Helen had been temporarily strained by Cyril's imperial pretensions, ill-feelings had passed with time, and the bride was especially devoted to her uncle and aunt. Above all, Ducky was a Princess of Great Britain by birth. The country represented a bastion of stability for her in a modern world where so much had foundered, most of all in her adopted Germany and Russia; and because of this she was proud to remember her English blood.

Ducky and Helen were sorry that Missy could not attend. 'If only you could have been here to share it all with us, what a joy it would have been,' Helen wrote to her from Buckingham Palace (25 November), shortly before Ducky's arrival. 'One longs for one's own generation in such moments, those with whom one has shared moments in the past and who remember and understand. For us it is like a dream finding ourselves in these surroundings again after all these last sad, drab years of exile – it is a mixed feeling of intense joy and sadness.'[4]

At the wedding itself on 29 November, in Westminster Abbey, Kira was one of the bridesmaids, an honour she shared with Princess Elizabeth of York, soon to find herself direct heir to the throne. Vladimir was one of the groomsmen at the Greek Orthodox ceremony which took place in the chapel at Buckingham Palace.

On the following day, Ducky and Cyril went to stay with Lord Howard de Walden and his family. A few days after their arrival, Ducky attended a grand party there. She had put on full evening dress and came downstairs when the party was in full swing. While engaged in a long conversation with one of the guests, she suddenly glanced down at her feet and found she was still wearing bedroom slippers.

After enjoying the Lord Howard de Waldens' hospitality, they went to stay with the Astors. Missy had been a close friend of Nancy Astor, the outspoken Conservative

Member of Parliament for the Sutton division of Plymouth, and her husband Waldorf, for over thirty years. Lord Astor took Cyril and Vladimir round the sights of London, including the Tower, Battersea Power Station, *The Times* printing works, the British Museum, and London Zoo. They attended luncheons in their honour at the German Embassy, and at the Astors' London residence, 4 St James Square.

It was significant that they had spent some time with the Astors, for Queen Marie of Roumania had asked them to keep a careful eye on her sister. Although Ducky and Cyril still outwardly gave the impression that nothing was wrong with their marriage, to their closest friends and relations it was apparent that Ducky was unhappy, perhaps even taking a perverse pleasure in her misery, despite the brave face which she displayed to the outside world.

From Dedinje, the Queen wrote to Lady Astor (13 December 1934):

> I am so glad you and Waldorf are looking after my
> poor sister. She needs helping and yet no one on
> earth is more difficult to help – All in her is
> overflowing bitterness & despair . . . I bless you for
> every kindness towards her, I am glad you
> understand her mental distress and how she needs
> to be helped in spite of herself – and he, poor ruin
> – it is all so sad and pathetic – and yet she is a
> great human being for all her mistaken ideas. She
> finds a sort of dreadful satisfaction in torment, she
> will not lift herself above her own misery nor will
> she ever admit that anybody else's point of view is
> right or even possible. She is the creature I love
> best in the world, I help her all I can but there is
> no help if she will not help herself. A really good,
> happy, comfortable, consoling time, could however

do her good, because she is so starved of all good
things – her life is fearfully melancholy, isolated &
depressing, and as you can see he is poor company!
The boy is delightful & Kira can be awfully nice, but
because of their humiliating position, she is always
on her defensive – God bless you for being kind &
helpful for these dear ones and I can never do
enough for, being so far . . . [5]

On the day after this letter was written, Ducky came
down to Plymouth with Nancy and Waldorf for the
weekend. It gave her what she may have realized was a
last chance to renew local associations of bygone days,
visiting haunts which she and her sisters had known so
well nearly half a century earlier. Admiralty House,
Devonport Dockyard, Mount Edgcumbe and Cotehele
had all changed little since the daughters of Devonport's
Commander-in-Chief had played, walked and swam
there. It must have struck her as ironic that these places,
like Windsor Castle and Buckingham Palace, had
remained barely untouched by the passage of time since
her father's day, while so much of Europe had altered
beyond recognition.

Though she continued to act as if nothing was wrong,
that Ducky's situation had not improved by the following
year was evident from a letter from Missy to Lord Astor,
written just after the sisters had stayed together at
Sonneberg (11 June 1935):

. . . We were very happy together and we talked
much, as much as we dared as neither of us
wanted to break down, and certain depths cannot
be touched without burning tears searing her
already tired eyes.

Her misery, both phisical [sic], mental, and
financial is so great that it has sapped her will-
power, she confessed this. Her problems and
difficulties are occasionally so devastatingly
crushing, and no one near to turn to, no one to
advise her, to stop in & help – to help her carry
her burden, no one efficient to discuss things, to
move, to act, only she herself, always, and never
any recognition and never any joy, that finally that
magnificent strong nature of yore, is tamed,
overcome, done with – This fills me with grief. She
never complains, it is only by short sentences torn
from her soul, in spite of herself, that I piece
things together – She needs a change, but it is no
good offering her a change or a holiday unless one
gets at her herself and arranges it for her. She is
neither financially nor mentally able to start, if you
understand my meaning . . . She lives with such
hopeless people, her husband being at the head of
the list, that she *cannot* move herself. Her strength
has run out, a sort of grey despair sets in, a feeling
that only death could liberate her from the
intolerable, crushing, overwhelming burden.
    As it is by what I give her that she lives, she has
the feeling that she *won't* ask more of me, even
when all gives out. Now I have made her swear,
that if she feels at the end of her tether that she
should send out a cry, that she should simply
telegraph 'Try and come' . . . Through the horror
of what happened to her in her married life, she
has learnt to doubt of all men; let us three at
least* teach her that this is wrong and let us try,
by continual effort, to show her that there are *some*
who feel & mean what they say . . . [6]

*Queen Marie herself, and Lord and Lady Astor.

Did Queen Marie's protectiveness towards her sister harbour some sense of guilt? It had saddened her that the close bond between them during childhood should have been strained by circumstances beyond their control. Missy had had the good fortune to be on the winning side for much of her life. Roumania, which had been under such threat from the Germans during the war, emerged triumphant after the armistice, with her territory considerably enlarged; and with her sheer force of personality and, it must be said, her sense of theatre, the Queen had been easily the most colourful member of Balkan royalty during the 1920s, fêted not only throughout Eastern Europe, but also in Britain and the United States of America. Not until her husband died and her son, King Carol, subjected her to endless personal humiliation had her luck really run out.

By contrast Grand Duchess Cyril had put a failed marriage behind her to marry again, been ostracized by her husband's sovereign for doing so, and when revolution struck, lost nearly everything. She had seen the country of her adoption, Russia, dragged into war and plunged into total chaos. It was not to be wondered at if relations between the 'jealous, unforgiving' sister who had been dealt such a cruel hand by fate, and her more fortunate sister, should have been complicated. Missy must have felt forever in her debt as a result.

In the winter, Cyril and Vladimir went to Paris, where the latter was to be coached for matriculation. They arrived on 8 December, but almost immediately Vladimir fell ill with whooping cough. Ducky herself came to Paris on 19 December. She was far from well at the time, but she had planned to go to Germany next day to see her elder daughter Marie, Princess of Leiningen, who was expecting a child. Mother and son were quite shocked to see how ill each other looked.

Shortly after her arrival in Wurzburg, Ducky contracted a

chill, but she would not hear of postponing the visit to her daughter. The birth of her granddaughter, Matilda, was not attended by any complications, and in the middle of January they all returned to Schloss Amorbach.*

That same week, Ducky was told that her cousin King George V was seriously ill at Sandringham, and his death was expected at any moment. He passed away on 20 January. 'I am so sorry for the dear King,' she remarked sadly. 'You know, we have rights on the Russian throne and some on the English; how splendid it would be if our two Empires could be joined, we would dominate the world.'[7]

By now she was steadily getting weaker, and the doctors were anxious. But by an immense effort of will, she attended the christening ceremony of her new grandchild. It taxed her strength considerably, and her condition continued to deteriorate. She suffered a stroke, one side of her body was paralyzed, and she was unable to speak coherently.

In February Kira was summoned to Amorbach, and Cyril and Vladimir were warned that she had taken a turn for the worse. They left at once to go to her bedside. Missy's daughter Ileana came to join the unhappy vigil. By the time they reached Ducky, she could only mutter occasional words which were barely intelligible.

There was nothing more the doctors could do. On the evening of 1 March they noticed a rapid weakening of the pulse. Missy, Sandra and Baby Bee all joined the bedside vigil, praying for her to go quickly and instead being tormented at the sight of her lingering. At fifteen minutes past midnight on 2 March, she passed away.

*Amorbach, where Marie and her family lived, was in a sense the cradle of the royal family. It had been the first married home of Edward, Duke of Kent, and his already once-widowed bride Victoire, Princess of Leiningen – the parents of Queen Victoria.

No more moving account of her last days and death can
be given than the description in Missy's letter to Lady
Astor (4 March):

The whole thing was tragic beyond imagination, a
tragic end to a tragic life.
    She carried tragedy within her – she had tragic
eyes – always – even as a little girl – But we loved
her enormously, there was something mighty about
her – she was our Conscience.
    But when he betrayed her, she did not know how
to forgive, so she allowed him to murder her soul.
From then onwards, her strength became her
weakness, her undoing – she was too absolute, she
could not overcome herself.
    And now she had to die, unforgiving! Her lips
were sealed because of the stroke which had felled
her to the ground – but although she knew we
were there and the first day she found a murmur of
recognition for each of us in turn, she shuddered
away from his touch – Whilst we sat, in turns
holding her hand, he stood like an outcast on the
threshold of her door not daring to enter her room –
    It took 11 long days before she was released.
The last five she lay in a sort of coma – and the
end came Sunday morning exactly at 12¼ –
suddenly it was all over, as she lay there grey,
gaunt, the mask of grief . . . it was torture – but I
am calm, I know it is better thus – she could not
have lived as a cripple – But with their egoism,
those she loved killed her. They left her too lonely
and she cried continually for three long years &
nothing brought her comfort nor resignation,
except occasionally her garden or her painting.
She would not let us help her. Her faith in
humanity was dead.

I know how much both you & Waldorf tried to
help her – she was deeply grateful, I know she was,
only her dreadful habit of never answering made
her case hopeless – In spite of our tremendous love
for each other, because of her silence, I was never
able to keep in touch with her, nor to really help
her – There is an unbearable tragedy in it all . . .[8]

Ileana saw her aunt's death as a blessed relief. 'The end
was thank God peaceful & though a great loss yet one
would be, in many ways, but thankful that she had passed
on to a happier relm [sic],' she wrote to Lady Astor. Kira,
she added, was 'quite broken & looks dreadful, I feel so
sorry for her just because she was often so hard, & now
she has nothing to go back to for help in herself or in
others . . . Mama is wonderful, so calm & quiet that she
does good to everyone only by just being there.'[9]

The sisters wrapped her body in a long white robe, and in
the coffin Missy placed white lilacs around her head and
shoulders. On 5 March, the coffin was brought to Coburg
and placed in the family vault of the Dukes of Saxe-
Coburg. The funeral took place next day, with rain and
snow flurries adding to the gloom of an icy winter scene,
as she was laid to rest beside her parents and brother.

Ducky had left a wish that there should be no pomp
and ceremony. Many relatives attended, but it was a
purely family affair, and there were no official representatives of the related royal houses. Apart from her sisters,
the guests included her niece Queen Elisabetha of
Greece, Charles, Duke of Saxe-Coburg and his family, the
ex-Tsar of Bulgaria with his daughter Eudoxia, Grand
Dukes Andrew and Dmitri Paulovich, and many representatives of Russian organizations.

Afterwards Missy found it hard to leave the grave of the

sister who 'always hated being alone'. As Meriel Buchanan would later write, the Grand Duchess Cyril died 'a bitter, disappointed woman, whose brilliant personality had been warped by failure and frustration'.[10] Now she was alone; but at last the 'passionate, often misunderstood child', who had grown up into a bitter, disappointed woman, was at peace.

Epilogue

Ducky's death was a severe shock to Cyril. To their son Vladimir, it seemed that for a long time he could not reconcile himself to the fact that she was dead. In every conversation he would always return to the one topic which really interested him – reminiscences of her. He would spend hours reading over her old letters and looking at her photographs. From that time onwards he devoted more and more time to their children, and when parted from any of them he was acutely lonely.

The arteriosclerosis, which had already started to make its effects felt, worsened, causing increasing problems with his circulation and eyesight, and later partial paralysis. Within a year of his wife's death, he was evidently a very sick man.

At Christmas 1937 their younger daughter Kira became engaged to Prince Louis Ferdinand of Prussia, second son of the ex-German Crown Prince, and grandson of the former Emperor. Though he was too ill to attend a reception at Paris in April 1938 organized in their honour, Cyril attended the wedding at Potsdam the following month. The Grand Duke of Mecklenburg-Schwerin had always been very sympathetic to Cyril and regarded him as head of the family, and because of the latter's straitened finances, he made a generous financial contribution towards the wedding costs. Cyril's health was visibly failing, and that summer he lingered on at St Briac, a virtual skeleton with bedsores, surrounded by memories of his married life.

He found some mental diversion in dictating his

memoirs, and completed eight chapters, taking the story to the outbreak of the revolution in 1917 and their departure from Russia. But it was becoming evident to his family that he had lost the will to live. Gangrene set in, and in September he was admitted to hospital in Paris. On 12 October 1938 he passed away in his sleep.

He thus outlived by three months the other person who had been closest to Ducky – her elder sister. Queen Marie of Roumania had made her will in 1933, leaving financial provision for her youngest daughter Ileana, and for the sister to whom she had given so much financial and moral support over the last few years. Ever since the war Missy had sent money and clothing, and helped with travel expenses, to her less wealthy sisters and mother until the latter's death. These were generous gestures which, after a while, she could ill afford. Although King Ferdinand had made ample provision for her before his death in 1927, their heartless and mercenary son King Carol had broken the terms of his father's will, appropriated his mother's income for himself and his mistress, and reduced her payment from the Roumanian civil list.

Ducky's first husband Ernie, Grand Duke of Hesse and the Rhine, had remarried, only a month after Ducky's wedding to Cyril – to Eleonore, Princess of Solms-Hohensolms-Lich. Despite his earlier homosexual tendencies, it was a success, and she bore him two sons. In October 1937 he died peacefully after a long illness. Not only was he spared the misery of a second European holocaust, but also a family tragedy which almost rivalled the massacre at Ekaterinburg in its sheer horror. Ernie's younger son Louis was engaged and preparing for his wedding in London the following month, and several of the wedding guests, including Louis's recently-widowed mother, elder brother and wife, boarded a plane from Frankfurt to Croydon three days before the ceremony was due to take place. While flying over Ostend they ran into thick fog, the plane hit a chimney stack, and crashed. None of the passengers or crew stood a chance of survival. The wedding took place in private, with the stunned bride and groom both dressed in black.

Neither Ducky nor Cyril had lived to a serene old age; their daughters, who never enjoyed particularly robust health, likewise died before their time. Like so many other descendants of Queen Victoria, Marie found her family life at the mercy of conflicting national loyalties in wartime. Her husband Prince Charles of Leiningen joined the German army, not so much out of enthusiasm for the Nazi cause, as out of a realization that any male German able-bodied citizen who did not express support for Hitler had the stark choice of fleeing the Fatherland, or being confronted by the Gestapo and eventually a concentration camp. He took part in the German invasion of Russia in 1941, and was captured by Russian forces at the end of the war. Two years later, a couple of German priests who had shared his captivity escaped from the camp, made their way to West Germany, and visited his wife with the sad news that in August 1946 he had been left to die of starvation, at the age of forty-eight. Left with six surviving children (a seventh had died two weeks after birth), his widow only survived him by five years. Shortly after arriving at Madrid on a visit to her brother in October 1951, Marie had a heart attack and died aged forty-four.

Kira, Princess Louis Ferdinand of Prussia since 1938, had a less troubled life. In 1940, Louis's elder brother, William, died in France of wounds received in battle. His funeral in Berlin was attended by quarter of a million people, and Hitler was alarmed at this display of national loyalty at the death of a man who would have been their future Emperor. Not wishing to see any more Hohenzollerns court the hero-worship in war that could undermine allegiance to the Nazi regime, he decided to retire all the princes of military age from active service. Louis Ferdinand was therefore discharged in 1941, a few months after his grandfather, the former Emperor William, had died. Although he and his wife had to move several times during the war, often to conditions of extreme discomfort, they avoided capture by the Nazis and Russians, and in 1947 settled in a house in Bremen, which has remained the family home ever since. In 1951 his father, the former Crown Prince William, died, and Louis Ferdinand was now head of the house of Hohenzollern. They had four sons and two daughters.

During her later years Kira suffered from high blood pressure. In September 1967, she and her husband visited her brother at St Briac. She was in her customary high spirits, and after doing justice to a splendid meal with her usual appetite, helped herself to several spoonfuls of white sugar in her coffee, exclaiming, 'God forbid I should eat anything healthy!' That evening she collapsed with a heart attack, and died the next day, aged fifty-eight.

Alone of the family, Grand Duke Vladimir reached the Biblical age of threescore years and ten. He attended the Russian High School in Paris and, despite his mother's apparent refusal to let him be educated in England, went on to the London School of Economics. His one brief spell of employment was in 1939, as a mechanic in Peterborough. For this purpose he assumed the name Mikhailov, the same as that which his ancestor Peter the Great used two centuries earlier while working in a Deptford shipyard. He spent much of the war in France, albeit under observation, resisting requests for help from the Nazis who attempted to trade on his parents' apparent sympathy for the movement in its early days. In 1944 he was forced by the Germans to leave St Briac, but they treated him with respect. The German officer in charge of his surveillance had orders not to let him fall alive into allied hands, and on being asked where he wished to go, he chose to stay with his sister Marie.

In August 1948 he married Princess Leonida, born Princess Bagration-Moukhransky. She was the widow of an American millionaire of Jewish blood, Sumner Moore Kirby, who had died a prisoner of the Nazis, leaving her with a small daughter. In 1953 she bore him a second daughter, who was later to marry Prince Francis William of Prussia, a great-grandson of Emperor William II.

Grand Duke and Duchess Vladimir divided their time between Paris, his parents' home in St Briac, and a villa in Madrid. Pressed in the late 1970s on the possibility of a restoration of the Russian monarchy, he replied that 'the only way of justifying our existence lies in being ready to serve our country and to do our duty if one day called upon to do so.' He disliked the term 'restoration' because of its retrogressive associations, preferring instead to speak of going 'forward to monarchy! While in my opinion all non-reigning European monarchy have equally remote chances, it must be said that monarchy is holding its own in Europe. It is a most convenient form of government, infinitely adaptable. It can accommodate every system, from complete dictatorial absolutism to complete democracy.' As for Russia, he admitted that a monarchy of the future would be a very different one from that which they had known in 1905 or 1917; 'it's the principle that counts, not the form.'

After the collapse of Communism in the USSR, he was at last permitted to visit his homeland, and travelled to St Petersburg in November 1991, but he was already in failing health. He collapsed and died on a visit to Miami, Florida, on 21 April 1992, aged seventy-five.

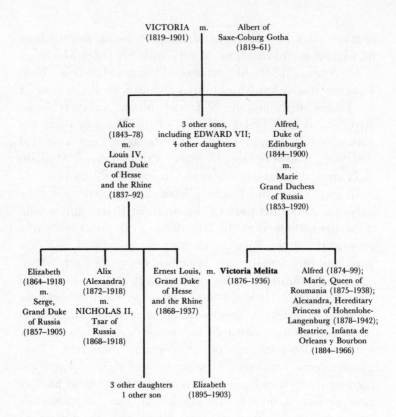

VICTORIA   m.   Albert of
(1819–1901)   Saxe-Coburg Gotha
                    (1819–61)

Alice   3 other sons,   Alfred,
(1843–78)   including EDWARD VII;   Duke of
m.   4 other daughters   Edinburgh
Louis IV,   (1844–1900)
Grand Duke   m.
of Hesse   Marie
and the Rhine   Grand Duchess
(1837–92)   of Russia
                                             (1853–1920)

Elizabeth   Alix   Ernest Louis, m. **Victoria Melita**   Alfred (1874–99);
(1864–1918)   (Alexandra)   Grand Duke   (1876–1936)   Marie, Queen of
m.   (1872–1918)   of Hesse   Roumania (1875–1938);
Serge,   m.   and the Rhine   Alexandra, Hereditary
Grand Duke   NICHOLAS II,   (1868–1937)   Princess of Hohenlohe-
of Russia   Tsar of   Langenburg (1878–1942);
(1857–1905)   Russia   Beatrice, Infanta de
                 (1868–1918)   Orleans y Bourbon
                                                                          (1884–1966)

                          3 other daughters   Elizabeth
                          1 other son   (1895–1903)

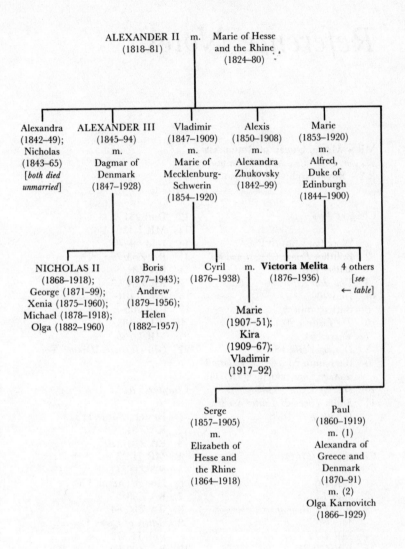

ALEXANDER II   m.   Marie of Hesse
(1818–81)   and the Rhine
                             (1824–80)

Alexandra   ALEXANDER III   Vladimir   Alexis   Marie
(1842–49);   (1845–94)   (1847–1909)   (1850–1908)   (1853–1920)
Nicholas   m.   m.   m.   m.
(1843–65)   Dagmar of   Marie of   Alexandra   Alfred,
[both died   Denmark   Mecklenburg-   Zhukovsky   Duke of
unmarried]   (1847–1928)   Schwerin   (1842–99)   Edinburgh
                                        (1854–1920)   (1844–1900)

     NICHOLAS II   Boris   Cyril   m. **Victoria Melita**   4 others
     (1868–1918);   (1877–1943);   (1876–1938) (1876–1936)   [see
     George (1871–99);   Andrew   ← table]
     Xenia (1875–1960);   (1879–1956);
     Michael (1878–1918);   Helen   Marie
     Olga (1882–1960)   (1882–1957)   (1907–51);
                                                             Kira
                                                             (1909–67);
                                                             Vladimir
                                                             (1917–92)

                    Serge   Paul
                    (1857–1905)   (1860–1919)
                    m.   m. (1)
                    Elizabeth of   Alexandra of
                    Hesse and   Greece and
                    the Rhine   Denmark
                    (1864–1918)   (1870–91)
                                                 m. (2)
                                                 Olga Karnovitch
                                                 (1866–1929)

Reference Notes

MR – Marie, Queen of Roumania
The story of my life (with volume no.)
RA – Royal Archives, Windsor

Chapter *1* *(pp. 1–13)*

1 Woodham-Smith 268
2 Bolitho, *Prince Consort and his brother* 170
3 *Your dear letter* 120
4 Ibid 200
5 Battiscombe 5
6 *The Listener* 20.11.1975
7 Vorres 54
8 *Darling Child* 132
9 Buchanan M., *Queen Victoria's relations* (henceforth *QVR*) 115
10 *Darling Child* 153–4
11 *Malta Times & United Services Gazette* 2.12.1876

Chapter *2* *(pp. 14–33)*

1 MR I 6
2 Ibid 4
3 Bolitho, *Biographer's notebook* 44
4 MR I 73
5 RA Z82/38
6 MR I 111–12
7 RA Z82/73
8 RA Z82/83
9 RA Z82/118
10 Pope-Hennessy 249
11 *Letters of Queen Victoria* Vol. I498

12 Duff 231
13 MR I 156
14 Ibid 69–70
15 RA Z83/75
16 RA Z84/3
17 RA Z84/67
18 MR I 181–2
19 Ibid 205–6
20 Pakula 33
21 MR I 208
22 Gill (*Western Morning News*)

Chapter *3* *(pp. 34–47)*

1 Hough, *Advice* 113
2 RA Z84/108
3 RA Z84/110
4 MR II 27
5 RA Z90/44
6 Hough, *Advice* 120
7 RA Z90/55
8 RA Z90/64
9 *Letters of Queen Victoria* Vol. II 372
10 RA Z90/69
11 *Empress Frederick writes to Sophie* 159
12 Pakula 100
13 *The Times* 19.4.1894
14 Ibid 20.4.1894
15 *Empress Frederick writes to Sophie* 170

Chapter *4* *(pp. 48-64)*

1 *Empress Frederick writes to Sophie* 180
2 Prince Nicholas of Greece 117
3 *Empress Frederick writes to Sophie* 201
4 Ibid 221
5 MR II 78
6 Ibid 78
7 Ibid 105
8 Bulow, *Memoirs 1897–1903* 482
9 Pakula 108
10 Hough, *Advice* 138
11 Cyril 73
12 Ibid 77

Chapter *5* *(pp. 65-78)*

1 Buchanan M., *QVR* 3–4
2 Mallet 167
3 Ibid
4 RA Z90/91
5 Ibid
6 RA Z90/97
7 Hough, *Advice* 147
8 *Letters of Queen Victoria* Vol. III 579
9 Longford, *Royal house of Windsor* 45
10 RA GV CC45/229
11 Pope-Hennessy 369
12 Hough, *Louis and Victoria* 209
13 Duff 263
14 Bing 157–8
15 RA CC29/40
16 Ernst Ludwig 56
17 Bulow, *Memoirs 1897–1903* 483

Chapter *6* *(pp. 79-93)*

1 Cyril 104
2 Ibid 112

3 Bibesco 160
4 Pakula 129
5 Cyril 123
6 Ibid 152–3
7 Ibid 153
8 Ibid 152
9 Ibid 174
10 Ibid 174
11 Ibid 182
12 Bulow, *Memoirs 1903–9* 168–70

Chapter *7* *(pp. 94–108)*

1 Cyril 184
2 Pakula 143
3 Astor Papers
4 Pakula 176
5 Massie 245
6 Bucharest Archives
7 Buchanan G. Vol. I 176–7
8 Bucharest Archives
9 Buchanan G. Vol. I 177
10 Buchanan M., *QVR* 199
11 Bucharest Archives
12 Buchanan M., *QVR* 199
13 Bucharest Archives
14 Cyril 187
15 Buchanan M., *QVR* 200–1
16 Bucharest Archives
17 MR II 329–32

Chapter *8* *(pp. 109–27)*

1 Cyril 194
2 Vorres 131
3 Cyril 198
4 Pakula 188
5 Buchanan M., *QVR* 201
6 Almedingen, *Alexandra* 109
7 MR III 107
8 Ibid 130
9 Cyril 205
10 Ibid 210
11 Ibid 210
12 Paléologue III 232

13 MR III 158
14 Cyril 211
15 Buchanan M., *QVR* 203
16 MR III 186

Chapter 9 *(pp. 128–47)*

1 McNaughton, *Flight* 130–31
2 MR III 127
3 McNaughton, *Flight* 131
4 Summers & Mangold 252; Warth 35
5 RA Add C22/206
6 RA Add C22/210
7 Bucharest Archives
8 Rowland 499
9 RA GV Q1550/XIX/319
10 RA GV Q1550/XIX/320
11 RA GV AA43/298
12 RA GV CC45/583

Chapter 10 *(pp. 148–70)*

1 Buchanan M., *QVR* 205
2 Vorres 171
3 Kurth 128
4 Ibid 82
5 Pakula 311
6 *The New York Times* 9.12.1924
7 Ibid 28.10.1924
8 Ibid 2.11.1924

9 Ibid 30.11.1924
10 Ibid 7.12.1924
11 Ibid 7.12.1924
12 Ibid 8.12.1924
13 Ibid 10.12.1924
14 Ibid 12.12.1924
15 Ibid 24.12.1924
16 Ibid 9.12.1924
17 Fenyvesi 253
18 Pakula 311
19 RA GV AA/43/314
20 Bucharest Archives
21 Ibid
22 Voules 30–31
23 Vorres 182
24 Cyril 233–4
25 Fenyvesi 251
26 Cyril 234

Chapter 11 *(pp. 171–84)*

1 Ponsonby 200
2 Pakula 392
3 RA GV CC45/934
4 Bucharest Archives
5 Astor Papers
6 Ibid
7 Private information
8 Astor Papers
9 Ibid
10 Buchanan M., *QVR* 206

Bibliography

I MANUSCRIPTS

Astor Papers, Reading University
Bucharest Archives
McNaughton, Arnold 'The flight of the Romanovs'
 – unpublished ms
Royal Archives, Windsor

II BOOKS

Almedingen, E.M., *The Empress Alexandra, 1872–1918: a study*. Hutchinson, 1961

— *An unbroken unity: a memoir of Grand Duchess Serge of Russia.* Bodley Head, 1964

Aronson, Theo, *Grandmama of Europe: the crowned descendants of Queen Victoria.* John Murray, 1973

Ashdown, Dulcie M., *Victoria and the Coburgs*. Robert Hale, 1981

Bibesco, Marthe Lucie, *Some royalties and a Prime Minister.* Appleton, 1930

Bing, Edward J. (ed), *The letters of Tsar Nicholas and Empress Marie: being the confidential correspondence between Nicholas II, last of the Tsars, and his mother, Dowager Empress Maria Feodorovna.* Ivor Nicholson & Watson, 1937

Bolitho, Hector, *A biographer's notebook*. Longmans, Green, 1950

— *The Prince Consort and his brother: two hundred new letters.* Cobden-Sanderson, 1933

Buchanan, Sir George, *My mission to Russia and other diplomatic memories,* 2 vols, Cassell, 1923

Buchanan, Meriel, *Ambassador's daughter.* Cassell, 1958

— *Queen Victoria's relations.* Cassell, 1954

Bulow, Bernhard, Prince von, *Memoirs 1897–1903.* Putnam, 1931

— *Memoirs 1903–1909.* Putnam, 1931

Cowles, Virginia, *The last Tsar and Tsarina.* Weidenfeld & Nicolson, 1977

Cyril, Grand Duke of Russia, *My life in Russia's service – then and now.* Selwyn & Blount, 1939

Daisy, Princess of Pless, *From my private diary.* John Murray, 1931

Dobson, Christopher, *Prince Felix Yusupov: the man who murdered Rasputin.* Harrap, 1989

Duff, David, *Hessian tapestry.* Muller, 1967

Elsberry, Terence, *Marie of Romania: the intimate life of a twentieth-century Queen.* Cassell, 1973

Ernst Ludwig, Grossherzog von Hessen und bei Rhein, *Erinnertes: mit einem biographischen Essay und Golo Mann herausgegeben von Eckhart G. Franz.* Eduard Roether Verlag, 1983

Fenyvesi, Charles, *Royalty in exile.* Robson, 1981

Fischer, Henry W., *The private lives of William II and his consort: a secret history of the court of Berlin.* Heinemann, 1904

Hough, Richard (ed), *Advice to a grand-daughter: letters from*

Queen Victoria to Princess Victoria of Hesse. Heinemann, 1975

— *Louis and Victoria: the first Mountbattens.* Hutchinson, 1974

King, Stella, *Princess Marina, her life and times.* Cassell, 1969

Kurth, Peter, *Anastasia, the life of Anna Anderson.* Jonathan Cape, 1983

Longford, Elizabeth, *The royal house of Windsor.* Weidenfeld & Nicolson, 1974

— *Victoria R.I.* Weidenfeld & Nicolson, 1964

McNaughton, Arnold, *Kings, Queens & Crowns.* Printed privately, 1977

Mallet, Victor (ed), *Life with Queen Victoria: Marie Mallet's letters from court 1887–1901.* John Murray, 1968

Marie, Queen of Roumania, *The story of my life,* 3 vols, Cassell, 1934–5

Massie, Robert K., *Nicholas and Alexandra.* Gollancz, 1968

Nicholas of Greece, Prince, *My fifty years.* Hutchinson, 1926

Pakula, Hannah, *The last romantic: a biography of Queen Marie of Roumania.* Weidenfeld & Nicolson, 1985

Paléologue, Maurice, *An Ambassador's memoirs,* (trans.) F.A. Holt, 3 vols, Hutchinson, 1923–5

Ponsonby, Arthur, *Henry Ponsonby, Queen Victoria's private secretary: his life from his letters.* Macmillan, 1942

Pool, James & Suzanne, *Who financed Hitler: the secret funding of Hitler's rise to power, 1919–33.* Raven, 1979

Pope-Hennessy, James, *Queen Mary, 1867–1953.* Allen & Unwin, 1959

Purnell's history of the 20th century, 9 vols, New Caxton Library Service, 1971–2

Radziwill, Princess Catherine, *The intimate life of the last Tsarina.* Cassell, 1929

Reid, Michaela, *Ask Sir James: Sir James Reid, personal physician to Queen Victoria and physician-in-ordinary to three monarchs.* Hodder & Stoughton, 1987

Rowland, Peter, *Lloyd George.* Barrie & Jenkins, 1975

Stephan, John J., *The Russian fascists: tragedy and farce in exile.* Hamish Hamilton, 1978

Summers, Anthony, & Mangold, Tom, *The file on the Tsar.* Victor Gollancz, 1976

Van der Kiste, John, & Jordaan, Bee, *Dearest Affie: Alfred, Duke of Edinburgh, Queen Victoria's second son.* Alan Sutton, 1984

Victoria, German Empress, *The Empress Frederick writes to Sophie, her daughter, Crown Princess and later Queen of the Hellenes: letters, 1889–1901,* (ed) Arthur Gould Lee. Faber, 1955

Victoria, Queen, *The letters of Queen Victoria, third series: a selection from Her Majesty's correspondence and journal between the years 1886 and 1901,* (ed) G.E. Buckle, 3 vols. John Murray, 1930–32

Victoria, Queen, and Victoria, Crown Princess, *Your dear letter: private correspondence between Queen Victoria and the Crown Princess of Prussia, 1865–1871,* (ed) Roger Fulford. Evans Bros, 1971

— *Darling child: private correspondence of Queen Victoria and the Crown Princess of Prussia, 1871–1878,* (ed) Roger Fulford. Evans Bros, 1976

Vorres, Ian, *The last Grand-Duchess: Her Imperial Highness Grand-Duchess Olga Alexandrovna, 1 June 1882–24 November 1960*. Hutchinson, 1964

Voules, Edward, *Free of all malice*. Printed privately, 1987

Warth, Robert D., *The allies and the Russian revolution: from the fall of the monarchy to the peace of Brest-Litovsk*. Cambridge University Press, 1954

Woodham-Smith, Cecil, *Queen Victoria, her life and times, Vol. 1, 1819–1861*. Hamish Hamilton, 1972

III PERIODICALS

The Listener
Malta Times & United Services Gazette
The New York Times
The Times

IV PERIODICAL ARTICLES

Gill, Crispin, 'Duchess was "too grand for Plymouth"' (Duchess of Edinburgh). In *Western Morning News*, 8 April 1985

Heu, Christoph, 'The controversial Grand Duchess' (Grand Duchess Vladimir, 1854–1920). In *The Monarchist*, January 1981

Index